HOME GROWN

Also by Joan Smith

The Loretta Lawson Crime Series

A Masculine Ending

Why Aren't They Screaming?

Don't Leave Me This Way

What Men Say

Full Stop

Other Fiction

What Will Survive

In Bed With (contributor), ed. Kathy Lette and others

Femmes de Siècle (ed.)

Non-fiction

Clouds of Deceit: The Deadly Legacy of Britain's Bomb Tests

Misogynies

Hungry for You: From Cannibalism to Seduction, a Book of Food

Different for Girls: How Culture Creates Women

Moralities: How to Stop the Abuse of Money and Power in the 21st Century

The Public Woman

Down with the Royals

HOME GROWN

How Domestic Violence
Turns Men Into Terrorists

Joan Smith

riverrun

First published in Great Britain in 2019 by riverrun

riverrun

An imprint of

Quercus Editions Ltd
Carmelite House
50 Victoria Embankment
London EC4Y 0DZ

An Hachette UK company

Copyright © 2019 Joan Smith

LONDON BOROUGH OF WANDSWORTH	
9030 00006 7326 4	
Askews & Holts	30-May-2019
303.625	£16.99
	WW18020962

A CIP catalogue record for this book is available
from the British Library.

Hardback ISBN 978 1 78747 604 2
Trade Paperback ISBN 978 1 78747 605 9
Ebook ISBN 978 1 78747 603 5

10 9 8 7 6 5 4 3 2 1

Typeset by CC Book Production

Printed and bound in Great Britain by Clays Ltd, Elcograf S.p.A.

Joan Smith is a novelist, columnist and human rights activist. She is the author of the feminist classic *Misogynies*, six novels and a number of polemics, most recently *Down with the Royals*. She has been co-chair of the Mayor of London's Violence Against Women and Girls Board since 2013.

'It may seem to some that this pattern of violence [terrorism] is different from violence against women and girls, but we in this place must recognise that the patterns of violent behaviour and the perpetration of violence against women and girls have been seen in the past history of many of those who go on to commit terrorist atrocities.'

Jess Phillips, MP for Birmingham Yardley,
House of Commons, 8 March 2018

'There was research in the 1980s ... the number one finding was that the first victim of an extremist or terrorist is the woman in his own home. We've forgotten that. We haven't built on that. Had we recognised them earlier as wife beaters and misogynists, I've no doubt that violence against women would have been a big flag when you have to decide who to carry out surveillance on.'

Nazir Afzal, former Chief Crown Prosecutor
for the North-west of England, in conversation
with the author, October 2018

Contents

Introduction

Terrorism is the scourge of our age. In Europe alone, in recent years, hundreds of people have been killed in attacks in France, Belgium, Spain, Germany, Sweden, Denmark and Norway. France has been particularly badly hit by a wave of shootings and suicide bombings, losing 130 people in a single night in November 2015, ninety of them at the Bataclan Theatre, where an American band was playing. Australia, Canada and the US have been attacked, along with Morocco, Tunisia, Turkey, Iraq, Iran and Afghanistan.

The UK was targeted in 2017 when the country suffered four fatal terrorist attacks in a three-month period, the first mass killings since fifty-two people were murdered in coordinated suicide bombings on the London transport system in the summer of 2005. Between March and June, people were killed on Westminster Bridge and at the entrance to Parliament, at the Manchester Arena as the audience left an Ariana Grande concert, on London Bridge and outside bars and restaurants in Borough Market, and outside a mosque at Finsbury Park. Three months after that, another terrorist exploded a home-made bomb on a Tube train at Parsons Green, in south London, causing a fireball and injuries but failing to kill anyone. In all, thirty-seven people died in these five attacks and hundreds were injured, many of them having to spend days or weeks in hospital, being treated for burns, stab wounds, crushed limbs or damage done by shrapnel.

But that wasn't the full picture of the terrorist threat to the UK: another *nine* plots were disrupted by the security services between March and December 2017 and the threat level remains 'severe', suggesting that another terrorist attack is judged to be 'highly likely'. As well as tracking would-be terrorists based in this country, counterterrorism police and the domestic security service, MI5, have had to deal with British men (and a small number of women) returning from conflict zones in the Middle East following the collapse of the terrorist group calling itself the Islamic State of Iraq and al-Sham (ISIS). Some of these individuals may simply go back to their old lives but others who want to come back, including two members of a notorious ISIS execution and torture squad known as 'the Beatles', are regarded as highly dangerous. Four hundred British jihad-ists have already returned, according to a Parliamentary debate in September 2018, but only forty have been prosecuted due to the difficulty of producing evidence of terrorist acts committed in countries where the rule of law had temporarily broken down. Police and MI5 have to keep an eye on all these individuals, whose numbers run into the thousands, and work out which of them pose an imminent threat in the UK. Trying to distinguish between angry young men who express heated anti-Western views and those who will actually plot terrorist attacks is the most urgent task facing the security services, and this book will suggest a new way – by understanding the close link between *private* and *public* violence – that it might be done.

At the same time, local authorities and other public bodies are trying to make bridges, shopping streets and landmarks safer from the kind of vehicle-based attacks that did so much damage in London in 2017. The task of keeping the public safe hasn't been so pressing since the height of the IRA bombing campaign on the mainland in the 1970s and '80s.

Most, but certainly not all, of the recent attacks have been jihadist in origin. In December 2017, a report into three of that year's attacks – Westminster Bridge, the Manchester Arena and London Bridge – offered rare insights into the thinking behind counterterrorism strategy, revealing a wealth of material that hadn't previously been in the public domain. (The Finsbury Park attack was excluded from the report because the perpetrator, Darren Osborne, was still awaiting trial when it was published.) Compiled by David (now Lord) Anderson QC, who had previously been the government's Independent Reviewer of Terrorism Legislation, it was based on an assessment of nine previously classified internal reviews which stretched to 1,150 pages. One of the most revealing sections was a comparison between the perpetrators of the three attacks and 269 individuals responsible for terrorist-related offences in the UK between 1998 and 2015. It was a large pool and revealed some striking common factors, including the fact that all five of the 2017 attackers under consideration were male, like 93 per cent of the larger total. (Female terrorists are not unknown but the overwhelming majority are male, like most of the individuals convicted of violent crimes in this country.)

The report also looked at nationality, revealing that almost three quarters of convicted terrorists (72 per cent) were British and around two fifths (43 per cent) lived in London. Perhaps more significantly, a substantial proportion (38 per cent) were already known to the police and almost half (48 per cent) had previously come to the attention of MI5. Slightly fewer (44 per cent) were already known to have links to a proscribed organisation, most often the Salafist terrorist group al-Muhajiroun. Supporters of ALM, which was founded by the hate preachers Omar Bakri Muhammad and Anjem Choudary, have been implicated in a number of terrorist operations, including a plot to attack the Ministry of Sound nightclub in London and the Bluewater shopping centre in Kent with fertiliser bombs, the murder of Fusilier Lee Rigby in south London in 2013 – and the Westminster Bridge and London Bridge attacks.

A much more striking connection between the 2017 attacks, as far as I was concerned, *wasn't* listed in the report. Four of the five attackers had a history of domestic abuse, amounting to a catalogue of verbal and physical attacks on female relatives and, in the case of the Manchester bomber, Salman Abedi, a brutal assault on a young woman who was in his class at college; the figure rises to five out of six if we include Osborne, the right-wing extremist who drove a hired van into worshippers leaving a mosque in north London. Less information has emerged about the family relationships of the remaining attacker, Khuram Butt, but we know that he displayed a somewhat detached view of fatherhood; Butt led the suicide attacks on London Bridge and Borough Market a matter of weeks after his wife had given birth to their second child. Another of the men in Butt's cell, Rachid Redouane, had a daughter aged seventeen months at the time he was shot dead by armed police, demonstrating a readiness to abandon infants which will figure in the biographies of a number of the perpetrators who appear in this book.

The patriarchal assumptions common among such men, who seek to control every aspect of the lives of their wives and children, extend neither to considering their long-term welfare nor to protecting them from the consequences of horrific public acts of violence. It is a chilling view of family relationships in which becoming a husband and father appears to have more to do with confirming a man's status – and acquiring residency rights, in some cases – than forming close attachments. The widows and children of terrorists have to live not just with grief and loss but with the notoriety of their male relatives, even in cases where they themselves were the first victims of an escalating species of male violence.

The wider pattern of terrorists with a history of domestic abuse certainly isn't limited to the UK: in the couple of years before the 2017 attacks, I kept noticing that the perpetrators of some of the most notorious terrorist attacks in Europe and the US had first been violent towards wives and girlfriends. Domestic violence turned up in the background of the security guard who attacked the Pulse nightclub in Florida (forty-nine dead, fifty-three injured), the lorry driver who drove into crowds in Nice on Bastille day (eighty-six dead, 458 injured), the elder of the two brothers responsible for the Boston marathon bombing (three dead, several hundred injured) and a fraudster who took hostages in a café in Sydney in December 2014 (two dead, three injured).

Critics will say that is to be expected, given that we are talking about a cohort of violent men, but that is my point: male violence doesn't stay in neat categories. Persistent offenders tend to have convictions for a whole range of violent offences, as I show in chapter two, and I'm suggesting that men who are used to beating, kicking, choking and stabbing women at home are considerably further along the road towards committing *public* acts of violence. Police and paramedics who have attended incidents of extreme domestic violence, coming upon a scene of injured women and children, pools of blood and overturned furniture, will recognise similarities with the aftermath of a marauding terrorist attack; these are men who have practised behind closed doors, relishing the sensation of holding the power of life or death over family members and becoming desensitised to the horrible effects of violence.

In the couple of years before I started writing this book, I waited in the aftermath of each succeeding terrorist outrage for details of the perpetrators' home lives to emerge, and I was surprised that so few commentators – myself and a handful of other feminist writers in this country and the US – had noticed or understood the significance of the overlap. I wrote about it in the *Telegraph* in the days after the Nice truck attack in 2016, arguing that 'a history of grudges against women and a record of domestic violence have been common factors in a number of such attacks, offering startling insights into the psychology of men who set out to kill complete strangers'.[1] A year later, following the London Bridge and Borough Market attacks, I returned to the theme in the *Guardian*,[2] providing brief details of the perpetrators' history and pointing out that the impact of domestic abuse is multigenerational; being exposed to parental violence as a child is now regarded as one of the principal adverse childhood experiences (ACEs) which have been implicated in a range of disastrous outcomes for boys, from involvement in gangs and street crime to abusing women themselves when they are older.

According to senior police officers, there is a striking similarity between boys who join gangs and those who are radicalised by propagandists for terrorist organisations such as Jabhat al-Nusra, the al-Qaeda affiliate in Syria more usually known as the al-Nusra Front, or ISIS. In some cases, they are the very same people, as I show in chapters four and five. Only a handful of abusive men will go on to become terrorists but the damage they do is long-lasting, disproportionate and has a huge impact on the wider community, as we saw in the moving scenes of mass mourning that took place in Manchester after the 2017 bombing.

One of the things I do, aside from being a writer, is chairing the committee at City Hall that draws up the Mayor of London's strategy to reduce violence against women and girls (the VAWG Board, for short). I've been co-chair since 2013 and I talk regularly to senior police officers, prosecutors, local politicians and representatives of women's organisations. In 2014, when Boris Johnson was Mayor, we began publishing maps of London showing incidents of rape, serious sexual assault and domestic violence in each of the thirty-two boroughs, using data on recorded crime from the Metropolitan Police. Unlike most of the general public, who seem unaware of how dire the situation is, I am staggered by the prevalence of violence towards women in London; it's one of the reasons why reports of domestic abuse leap out at me when I read about men who've committed other violent crimes, such as terrorism.

Towards the end of 2017, in a meeting with one of the country's most senior police officers, I asked whether he'd noticed that the London and Manchester terrorist attacks were all carried out by men who'd abused women. He reacted with genuine surprise, saying that the connection had never come up, not even once, in any of the discussions he'd had over many years with experts on terrorism. The next time I saw him, he said he had gone straight back to his office and asked whether there was any data or analysis identifying terrorists with a history of domestic violence. There wasn't, he discovered. 'Intellectually, we're sure you're right,' he told me, 'but we don't have the data.' It still didn't exist, last time I asked, which was during the writing of this book.

That doesn't surprise me, in light of the invisibility of most male violence, a subject I address at greater length in the final chapter of this book. To my knowledge, there isn't a definitive list of terrorists with a history of domestic abuse prior to their attacks on members of the public, but that is because no one has ever tried to produce one. If you go to a bookshop, you will find shelves groaning under the weight of old and brand-new books on terrorism, charting the rise of the Taliban, al-Qaeda (AQ) and ISIS, but domestic violence almost never appears in an index. Neither, astonishingly, does misogyny: most commentators seem to have overlooked the fact that hatred of women and a history of domestic violence are key indicators of dehumanisation, a process of seeing other people as objects, which is a necessary first step towards becoming a terrorist. To their credit, some authors *have* addressed the subject of sex slavery and sex trafficking by the leaders of ISIS, but the discussion is usually limited to the scarcely imaginable torture and enslavement suffered by Yazidi women in Iraq and Syria. It's all the more perplexing because misogyny, and the acceptability of rape and domestic violence, are fundamental to the ideology of ISIS – not to mention a recruiting tool, as I explain later in the book.

But it's important to point out here that jihadists don't have a monopoly on misogyny or mistreating women, no matter how much their activities have come to dominate the news agenda in recent years. There is a growing threat in this country from right-wing extremists such as the Finsbury Park terrorist and the Nazi sympathiser who murdered the Labour MP Jo Cox, and some of them share a history of extreme misogyny with the Islamists who are their ideological enemies. The far right is usually regarded as a distinct phenomenon from religious fundamentalism but many angry white men, as well as displaying predictable traits of racism and homophobia, are dyed-in-the-wool woman-haters who have spent years beating up female relatives in their own homes. The same pattern is even more pronounced among mass killers in the US, where the easy availability of guns has encouraged the growth of a lethal species of toxic masculinity. Defenders of lax gun laws, who include Donald Trump, usually fail to mention that some of the most notorious mass murders in the US began with fatal assaults on the female relatives in the shooter's own home, as I show in chapter seven.

It's only a minority of men who pose a threat, but we urgently need ways of identifying highly dangerous individuals at an earlier stage. My argument in this book is that a history of domestic violence should be one of the highest risk factors but we can't just leave it to the police and security services, who are dealing with the end stage of a process that's been going on for years. We are confronted by an epidemic of violence against women in this country, yet its scale and effects are played down or even denied altogether. That's because of an insidious perception that there are reasons – long-standing, understandable and therefore excusable – for some men to hurt women. It goes without saying that any such notion should be intolerable in a society that claims to believe in equality between the sexes. But, as this book will show, the failure to acknowledge the extent of violence against women has had unforeseen consequences in an area of criminal activity not previously associated with hatred of women.

In the final chapter, I make some suggestions about how we should go about tackling this epidemic of male violence. I make no apology for being both feminist and polemical: if we want to stop terrorist attacks and mass murder, we have to get much more serious about recognising the profoundly misogynistic violence that's going on behind closed doors.

1

The Unassuageable Rage of the Kouachi Brothers

'No one kills over a caricature'

The first Wednesday of 2015 began as a perfectly ordinary morning. I was working at home in London when news alerts of a terrorist attack in Paris began to arrive on my mobile phone. I knew that the city hadn't been the target of a fatal terrorist attack since the middle of the 1990s when the Métro was bombed by jihadist groups linked to the civil war in France's former colony, Algeria. There *had* been a spate of shootings in south-west France in 2012, carried out by a French-Algerian man called Mohammed Merah and resulting in the deaths of seven people, but everyone had hoped it was a one-off. So breaking news of a mass shooting in Paris – and in a newspaper office, where journalists had gathered for a routine editorial conference – was hugely alarming.

According to early reports, the target was a weekly newspaper called *Charlie Hebdo*, founded in 1970 and one of the products of the secular, left-wing, anticlerical revolt that shook France a couple of years earlier. It was known for its satirical approach to politics and religion, and while it didn't treat Islam more harshly than Catholicism, it had published cartoons ignoring the prohibition on representations of the Prophet Muhammad. As a secular journalist and campaigner for free expression, I had written columns in its defence when its offices were firebombed four years earlier, and I knew that the editor, Stéphane Charbonnier (better known under his pen name, Charb), had been under police guard ever since. Another attack was always on the cards, but the reports coming out of Paris sounded like carnage: two masked men walking into the newspaper office, shouting, *'Allahu akbar . . . Where is Charb?'* and opening fire with assault rifles and machine pistols. Soon the hashtag *#jesuischarlie* was trending on Twitter, where updates on the attacks were being posted by individuals and news organisations. As the day wore on, a horrific amateur video was uploaded to the Internet, showing the terrorists murdering a wounded police officer, who was obviously of north African heritage, in the street outside the newspaper office. By the evening, the extent of the massacre – twelve dead and eleven injured, some of them seriously – was horribly clear.

But that wasn't the end of the incident: the terrorists had been identified and were on the run, becoming the most wanted men in France, while a second spate of shootings, carried out by an associate, was under way in the city. Over the next two days, a policewoman was shot dead, four people were murdered in a Jewish supermarket at Porte de Vincennes, in the east of the city, and all three terrorists were killed, in two separate shoot-outs, on Friday evening. On Sunday, millions of people joined the French President, François Hollande, and world leaders in a march across Paris in solidarity with the seventeen people killed in the attacks.

I have had a particular horror of terrorist attacks since 1999, when I walked past a pub in Soho about ten minutes before it was blown up by a nail bomb planted by a British neo-Nazi. I had barely arrived in a nearby bar when the explosion shook the windows looking on to the street, reminding me instantly of a terrorist attack in the Grand Bazaar in Istanbul five years earlier, when a bomb planted by a Kurdish terrorist organisation, the PKK, exploded and killed three people. In Soho, everyone rushed to the windows of the bar, not realising what had just happened, and I shouted at them to get back in case there was a second bomb. Then I ran into the street with a friend, with some vague notion that we might be able to help, and headed towards the corner of Old Compton Street, which was the direction the noise had come from.

We were faced by a scene of utter devastation: broken glass littered the street, clouds of dust drifted in the air and a motorbike lay on its side in the middle of the road, the wheels still turning. The most striking thing was the eerie silence, in contrast to the sound of the detonation a couple of minutes earlier. I heard no screams, couldn't work out what the source of the blast was, and it took me a moment to notice the figure of a man standing on a corner, his chest and arms bare. It was an unseasonably warm April evening and I remember thinking he was brave, going out without a shirt, until it dawned on me that his clothes had been blown off the upper part of his body.

At that moment, a uniformed police officer appeared and shouted at us to get back, yelling something about a second device. We dived into a bar and remained there while casualties from the Admiral Duncan pub were wheeled past the windows, on their way to a field hospital which was being set up in Soho Square. Eventually the staff pulled down the blinds, shielding us from the torment of having to watch without being able to help, but no one was allowed to leave until the police declared the incident over, two or three hours later. When we emerged, central London was still in lockdown, with buses and Underground trains stopped, and we had a long walk before we could find a taxi. By then, the symptoms of shock were kicking in, feelings of numbness and hyperventilation caused by a surge of adrenaline, and I came down with a heavy cold a couple of days later.

I followed the news avidly, discovering that three people had been killed in the blast and many others had terrible injuries, including loss of limbs, caused by the nails packed into the bomb. I was enormously relieved when the police made an arrest a couple of days later and the suspect, twenty-two-year-old David Copeland, was eventually convicted of murder and sentenced to life in prison. I wasn't close enough to witness the attack, but hearing the detonation and seeing the immediate aftermath was enough to cause nightmares. I had recurring dreams about shattered glass raining down on my head, I was gripped by panic attacks in enclosed places and I couldn't stay in an unfamiliar space until I'd identified the emergency exits. I was eventually diagnosed with a form of post-traumatic stress disorder (PTSD) and I got used to the fact that the symptoms returned each time there was another terrorist attack, such as the Bali nightclub bombing in 2002 and the 7/7 suicide attacks in London in 2005.

Because the targets were journalists, I had a particularly strong reaction to the *Charlie Hebdo* attack. Earlier in my own career, I'd sat in hundreds of editorial meetings at the *Sunday Times* and the *Independent on Sunday*, and I was transfixed at the thought of such a gathering, where ideas are kicked around and jokes made, being turned into a scene of carnage. I wrote an angry piece for the *Guardian* website on the afternoon of the attack, arguing that the answer to journalists being silenced had to be more journalism. I desperately wanted to know who had done this truly terrible thing and I followed the news as closely as I had after the Soho bombing, although the Internet means that facts are quicker to emerge these days than they were in 1999.

Soon we had basic information about the perpetrators: the *Charlie Hebdo* attack was carried out by two French-Algerian brothers, Saïd and Chérif Kouachi, aged thirty-four and thirty-two, while the supermarket murders were the work of their friend, Amedy Coulibaly, also thirty-two, whose parents were from the former French colony of Mali in west Africa. The fact that all three were born in France prompted an anguished debate about a new species of 'home grown' terrorism, which now appeared to have begun with the rampage of the Toulouse terrorist, Mohammed Merah, three years earlier. There was an intense discussion of radical Islam in France, with some experts identifying a new species of recruiting campaign aimed at angry young Muslims of French origin, while others argued that racism, poverty and systemic discrimination should be in the frame. I didn't think these explanations were necessarily wrong or even mutually exclusive, but I also didn't think they were sufficient explanation for the extreme acts of violence carried out by the brothers.

Like the 7/7 bombers, who left behind 'martyrdom' videos showing themselves in military-style fatigues, the Kouachi brothers and their accomplice, Coulibaly, were acting out a fantasy of being soldiers. Their behaviour, dressing up in masks and body armour like a home-made version of special forces kit, resembled a scene from a video game or the latest

Hollywood blockbuster – simultaneously ridiculous and lethal. They couldn't even agree among themselves which jihadist organisation they were killing for: Saïd and Chérif Kouachi claimed to be acting on behalf of AQ in the Arabian Peninsula (AQAP) but their co-conspirator, Coulibaly, left behind a video declaring his allegiance to its deadly rival, ISIS. It seemed odd to me that this contradiction, which should have made them mortal enemies, hadn't caused friction at the planning stage, especially as Coulibaly's belongings included the sinister black ISIS flag flown by lorry-loads of jihadists on their way into Raqqa and Mosul.

But that was far from being the only incoherent aspect of the attacks: the Kouachi brothers were so invested in their military fantasy that they boasted, in a bizarre telephone interview one of them gave during the stand-off with police, about following a code of honour which didn't allow them to kill women or fellow Muslims. Yet everyone who watched the dreadful amateur video filmed outside the office had seen them murder a Muslim police officer, Ahmed Merabet, and minutes before that they shot dead a woman, the psychoanalyst and columnist Elsa Cayat, in the *Charlie Hebdo* office. None of this made sense, even in the dangerous internal world of young men imagining themselves as religious warriors, but the most pressing problem lay in their motivation.

No one, it seems to me, carries out an extremely bloody massacre over a cartoon. True, some of the young men carrying out murders in the name of religion or ideology *claim* that is why they are doing it, and I'm sure they have convinced themselves. Kurt Westergaard, the Danish cartoonist who in 2005 drew a controversial image of the Prophet Muhammad with a bomb in his turban, in a deliberate test of the limits of free expression, narrowly escaped death five years later when a Somali jihadist armed with a knife and an axe broke into his home, intent on killing him. But the fact remains that millions of Muslims in France were offended by *Charlie Hebdo*'s satirical approach to their religion without feeling the need to get military training at a terrorist camp in Yemen, acquire assault rifles and murder a dozen people in cold blood.

The more interesting question is why some men (they almost always are men, as we saw from MI5's analysis of convicted terrorists in the UK, in the introduction) are so susceptible to violent ideology. It certainly wouldn't have been difficult to put extreme ideas into the mind of Coulibaly, a man with a long criminal record for armed robbery and drugs offences who was introduced to the violent world of radical Islam in prison; a psychiatric report ordered by a court in 2013, after one of Coulibaly's numerous arrests, concluded that he had an 'immature and psychopathic personality', a diagnosis supported by the way he casually paused to make himself a sandwich after shooting four people dead during the attack on the supermarket. But the Kouachi brothers had no such diagnosis and their closest living relative, their sister Aicha, poured scorn on their claimed motivation for the *Charlie Hebdo* murders when she was interrogated by the French police and security services.

'*Non, on ne tue pas pour un dessin,*'[3] she declared – no one kills over a caricature. She suggested that her brother Chérif had been 'saving face' – hiding another motive which he would have been reluctant to acknowledge – when he claimed to be avenging the Prophet.

Brothers in arms vs toxic masculinity

It is a striking fact, according to survivors of the attack, that Saïd and Chérif Kouachi didn't burst into the *Charlie Hebdo* office, guns blazing and spraying bullets everywhere. On the contrary, they behaved like executioners, asking for individuals by name, witnessing the terror on their faces as they realised they were the next to die and picking them off with single shots. They relished being in control of the situation, wielding the power of life and death over their defenceless victims, as this description of the confrontation between one of the gunmen and a survivor, the journalist Sigolène Vinson, illustrates:

The gunman told her: 'Don't be afraid, calm down, I won't kill you.' He spoke in a steady voice, she said, with a calm look in his eyes, saying: 'You are a woman. But think about what you are doing. It's not right.' Then she said he turned to his partner, who was still shooting, and shouted: 'We don't shoot women! We don't shoot women! We don't shoot women!'[4]

This is a man deep inside his role play, lecturing the 'enemy' and laying claim to a code of chivalry which doesn't permit the murder of women (although, as we know, one of the brothers ignored it). It's also classic victim-blaming, something often witnessed during outbursts of male violence, whether the perpetrator is a terrorist, a rapist telling his victim he'll spare her if she doesn't struggle or a husband explaining to his terrified wife that his violence is all *her* fault.

In the days after the massacre, I was astonished that so little attention was being paid to this aspect of the *Charlie Hebdo* attacks, as though the sex of the perpetrators was purely incidental. I said as much in a column published on the weekend after the attack, pointing out that it had never occurred to me for a single moment that the terrorists would turn out to be women. I compared the Kouachi brothers to mass murderers in the US, such as the Sandy Hook killer, Adam Lanza, and Elliot Rodger, perpetrator of a marauding attack in Isla Vista, California. I wrote:

There is a pattern here of troubled men projecting their self-hatred on to other people: fellow students, women, novelists, journalists, Jews, Muslims. They display a sense of aggrieved entitlement which over-rides any possibility of empathy with their victims; acquiring an arsenal of Kalashnikovs and grenade-launchers offers a feeling of power which they seldom experience in their everyday lives [. . .]

Did the Kouachi brothers delude themselves that they

were proving their manhood when they burst out of the print works on Friday afternoon, guns blazing, and died in a hail of bullets? The striking thing about such men is that they are drawn to a toxic form of identity which equates masculinity with violence.[5]

I was still in shock when I wrote this column and I didn't have space to address the question of why Saïd and Chérif Kouachi were so troubled, other than to point out that they had been unemployed or doing unskilled jobs for most of their adult lives. I knew that they were orphans, who had spent time in the French care system, and that many 'looked-after' children emerge from state institutions with few qualifications and bleak prospects. It seemed to me that the roots of their violence as adult men were likely to lie somewhere in this background, explaining why they had become so susceptible to the hate-filled rhetoric of a series of Salafist imams.

Few people asked this crucial question in the rush to catalogue the admittedly extensive connections between the Kouachi brothers and radical Islam, which went back a decade and a half. It emerged from briefings by the Paris prosecutor, François Molins, and a mass of documents obtained by journalists in the wake of the massacre, that the brothers had been radicalised by a series of male mentors, beginning with a fiery young imam, Farid Benyettou, at a mosque in north-east Paris, not far from where they had grown up. Benyettou was the leader of what became known as the Buttes-Chaumont terrorist network, named after the park in Paris where its members trained for jihad, and he sent a number of young men to fight the Americans in Iraq. Chérif Kouachi was more interested in staging terrorist attacks in Paris but he didn't want to lose face with other members of the group. He was arrested in January 2005, shortly before he was due to board a flight to Damascus and make his way across the border into Iraq. He spent the next twenty months awaiting trial in the huge Fleury-Mérogis prison, to the south of Paris, which held so many Islamists that it was becoming known as a recruiting ground for would-be jihadists. Here Chérif met both Coulibaly, who was serving a sentence for armed robbery, and Djamel Beghal, a high-ranking member of AQ who had trained in camps in Afghanistan. Beghal, who had been convicted of plotting to blow up the American embassy in Paris, made a big impression on Coulibaly and Chérif Kouachi, who appeared to be a much more committed Islamist when he was released from prison in 2006. He got married in 2008 and took his new wife on a honeymoon trip to Saudi Arabia, after which she gave up her job as a nursery assistant and started to appear fully veiled in public.

On the face of it, Chérif was more directly involved with Islamists that his elder brother but the following year Saïd lost his job as a member of a team which knocked on doors to promote recycling schemes; he was said to be part of a group of city employees who followed a strict version of Islam, bringing prayer mats to work and flatly refusing to shake hands with women. Chérif, meanwhile, remained in contact with some of the jihadists he had met in prison and in 2011 he met his third mentor, the notorious Yemeni-American cleric Anwar al-Awlaki, on a clandestine trip for military training in Yemen. Documents found by the police on his computer in 2010, during an investigation into a plot to help a convicted terrorist escape from prison in France, suggest that Chérif was already thinking about, if not actually planning, a terrorist attack similar to the shootings at the *Charlie Hebdo* office. He didn't put it into action immediately, possibly because Saïd wasn't yet fully on board; it would take another four or five years before both brothers were ready to stage the attack Chérif had long fantasised about. But even within this narrative, which is on the face of it all about radical Islam, there are clues to the profound psychological damage they were carrying around.

Their sister Aicha described them as 'very racist' towards anyone who wasn't Arab or Muslim. Chérif in particular was virulently anti-Semitic, talking endlessly to other members of the Buttes-Chaumont network about attacking Jewish shops or firebombing a synagogue in Paris. Hatred of Jews was one of the brothers' prime motivations – Elsa Cayat, the only woman murdered by the Kouachis, was Jewish, and her family believe that was the reason why she was singled out when other female members of staff survived. It could hardly be more obvious that anti-Semitism was the motivation of their accomplice, Coulibaly, who deliberately attacked a Jewish supermarket two days after the *Charlie Hebdo* massacre.

Both brothers were openly misogynistic, with Chérif displaying his contempt for women by refusing to stand up in court because the case against him was being heard by a female judge. He loved the conspiratorial world of radical Islam, holding clandestine meetings in the countryside with other jihadists and fantasising about himself as a warrior when he was actually driving round Paris, delivering pizzas. The truth is that both brothers were volatile, angry young men *before* they came under the influence of Salafist Islam, and their background involved several of the adverse childhood experiences (ACEs) I mentioned in the introduction – including domestic violence.

Saïd and Chérif Koauchi were born in 1980 and 1982 to parents who emigrated to France from Algeria. Mokhtar Kouachi and Freiha Meguireche had two other children: their daughter Aicha, who was born between Saïd and Chérif, and a younger boy, Chabane. The children spent their infancy in the Nineteenth arrondissement of Paris, classic *banlieue* territory next to the ring road and popular with immigrant families because of its low-cost social housing. A few years later, as unrest erupted in the suburbs of Paris and other French cities, the then Interior Minister (and later President) Nicolas Sarkozy caused outrage when he described the rioters as *'racaille'*, a hugely pejorative term which translates as 'rabble'. Racism, poverty and low expectations are part of the story of the *banlieues*, creating a generation that grew up with very different attitudes towards their home country than their parents. Professor Gilles Kepel, one of the foremost experts on contemporary jihadism, has argued that deprivation in these communities created fertile ground for foreign organisations such as ISIS:

> France has been an especially tempting target because of the disastrously high unemployment rate among young people from immigrant backgrounds who live in the banlieues. The largely Arabic-speaking North African provenance of these children of immigrants – an echo of French colonial history – is a boon for Arab jihadist recruiters, who target this community in particular.[6]

This is certainly not the only story to emerge from the Paris *banlieue,* which has produced national heroes such as France's 2018 football World Cup star, Kylian Mbappé. His mother and father, whose roots were in Algeria and Cameroon respectively, were accomplished sports players and brought him up in Bondy, a poor town on the north-east edge of Paris, just a few miles up the road from the Nineteenth arrondissement.

But there is no denying that Rue d'Aubervilliers, where the Kouachi parents settled to bring up their growing family, was a world away from the luxury apartment blocks of central Paris. The neighbourhood was run-down, inhabited by families with few choices, and social workers were daunted by the scale of the problems they faced and a shortage of the resources needed to tackle them. After the *Charlie Hebdo* attacks, several former neighbours came forward to talk about the problems faced by the Kouachi family, including the fact that Freiha Meguireche was left to raise the children on her own after her husband walked out or died; there were lurid stories about her being so poor that she had to sell sex to put food on the table at the end of the month. In reality, Mokhtar Kouachi died of cancer in 1991, when Saïd and Chérif were eleven and nine. Losing a parent in childhood is a traumatic event but in this instance, grief for their loss would have been complicated by the fact that their father was a violent bully.

'My father used to beat us, my mother neglected us,'[7] Aicha told the police in interviews after the massacre. She said he hadn't distinguished between the children – they all suffered equally – but we know that the impact of domestic violence is affected by sex and position in the family. It is likely that the two eldest boys, growing up in a patriarchal family, would have borne the brunt of their father's violence and felt humiliated by it. After his death, their mother had a fifth child, Salima, by another man, earning the disapproval of her conservative Muslim neighbours and possibly giving rise to the rumour that she was involved in prostitution.

Whatever the truth of that, Freiha Meguireche's health was poor and she received little financial support from the state, unable even to pay for the children's school lunches. A neighbour, Evelyne, who set up an organisation to provide food and days out for children from deprived families, provided a vivid portrait of the children at this time to a French website, Reporterre, describing how they began to look thin and neglected. When she took the brothers on a trip to Euro

Disney, she noticed that Chérif was tense and on edge – like milk boiling on a stove, she said – but when she got to know him, she was surprised by what she found: 'I loved that boy. All it took was someone to make a fuss, to give him a cuddle, and he calmed down.'[8] In a revealing insight into the brothers' relationship, she recalled Saïd 'whining' all the time and following his brother everywhere, as if he, not Chérif, was the younger brother. Despite her efforts, the boys were bullied, and she once witnessed a caretaker forcing Chérif to his knees and making him apologise for some minor offence. She described the younger boy as a '*souffre-douleur*', an evocative phrase that translates as a whipping boy or punchbag.

Domestic violence, neglect, humiliation: this was the everyday life of the two oldest Kouachi boys and it's not surprising that they formed a united front against the world. 'My brothers, they were like a couple,'[9] Aicha told the police. It is a striking fact that pairs of brothers have been over-represented in recent terrorist attacks: as well as the *Charlie Hebdo* massacre, they featured in the Boston marathon bombing in 2013; the coordinated attacks on a football stadium and the Bataclan theatre in Paris in November 2015; the bombing of the main airport and an underground station in Brussels in March 2016; and the marauding attacks in Catalonia in August 2017. Close family relationships have a reinforcing effect, allowing young men who encounter extremist ideology to explore it within an atmosphere of absolute trust – and, in the case of the Kouachi brothers, the bond was formed at an early age.

It would have been strengthened in 1994, when Freiha Meguireche's health got worse and she was forced to acknowledge that she could no longer support all five of her children; very reluctantly, she asked social services to take over care of the two elder boys, assuming that she would be able to bring them home when her health improved. What happened next was extraordinary: instead of finding accommodation for Saïd and Chérif with foster parents or at a children's home in Paris, social workers sent them deep into rural France, to the village of Treignac in Corrèze, 300 miles south of Paris. A quarter of a century later, rural France still tends to be white and mono-cultural, and the picturesque village of Treignac had a population of only 1,400 at the time. It was a world away from the crowded, multicultural area of Paris where the brothers had grown up, and too far for their mother to visit them, even if she could have found the train fare. But the move went ahead and, in the autumn of 1994, the brothers arrived at the Monédières centre, run by the charitable Claude Pompidou Foundation, and joined around seventy other children with social and behavioural problems. Children from the centre were easily identifiable when they walked through the village in groups, marking them out as outsiders, and that was especially true of two Muslim boys from a north African family. How they felt about being sent so far from home, and to a place where they so obviously stood out, is not hard to imagine – and it would have compounded their feelings of rejection by their mother, even though it was not her choice to send them hundreds of miles from the rest of their family.

Freiha Meguireche often rang the centre to speak to her elder sons but by now she was seriously ill, and terrified to go into hospital because she feared losing the three children who were still at home. In January 1995, Aicha came home from school at lunchtime to find her mother lying dead on the kitchen floor. The cause of death was said to be a drug overdose, possibly deliberate. The news was relayed to her brothers, who had not seen their mother for several months, by phone. They were twelve and fourteen, and were now officially orphans.

Mass murderers, self-hatred and suicide

Nothing about this tragic story excuses what the Kouachi brothers did. Many children, including siblings from the same families, grow up in equally damaging circumstances but don't become abusers, let alone terrorists. Resilience varies from one individual to the next, and the influence of a trusted adult from inside or outside the family may make all the difference, but Saïd and Chérif Kouachi appear to have lacked both. Without positive role models, it is not surprising that they were susceptible as young adults to malign forms of influence, such as the hate preachers who were on the lookout for recruits when the brothers eventually returned to the suburbs of Paris.

In the meantime, and not long after their mother's death, they were joined at the Monédières centre by their siblings. With the whole family now transported to Treignac, there were brief hopes of a reunion, but it didn't last long because the younger children, Chabane and Salima, were soon found foster homes. The brothers and Aicha remained at the centre, where Chérif threw himself into football and entertained dreams of becoming a professional player, but there was a darker side to his nature. He was a show-off and acquired a reputation for being quick to use his fists, on one occasion beating up a new boy on his first day at the centre, for no obvious reason. His school reports were poor, something that might have been connected to low expectations on the part of some of his teachers, but he rejected support from staff who tried to help him with academic subjects. They didn't remember either boy being particularly religious but while Saïd was more reserved and worked harder at school than his younger brother, he shared Chérif's hostility towards any form of authority.

The atmosphere at the centre deteriorated markedly in 1997 when it began to accept children sent by the criminal courts. During their final years in Treignac, the brothers were exposed to brawls, petty thefts and drug dealing – experience Chérif would make use of when he found himself unemployed in Paris three years later. Saïd was old enough to leave the centre when he reached eighteen in 1998 but by now the two boys were used to presenting a joint face to the world. Reluctant to be parted from his younger brother, Saïd asked if he could stay on to complete a catering course while Chérif took sports studies and electrical engineering at a nearby college. In the event, Chérif got into fights with the staff and left without finishing either.

In 2000, aged eighteen and twenty, the brothers left Treignac and returned to Paris for the first time since their mother's death. Chérif stayed with relatives at first but he was kicked out and ended up sleeping on friends' sofas and on the streets, his dreams of becoming a professional footballer rapidly evaporating. Using some of the unofficial knowledge he had picked up from boys at the centre, he supported himself through petty theft and drug dealing until a friend offered both brothers a place to stay in their old stamping ground, the Nineteenth arrondissement.

The place had changed: they soon found themselves living among young men, born and brought up in France, who had found a new sense of identity in a radical version of Islam. When Saïd persuaded Chérif to go with him to a mosque, they were easy pickings for a charismatic imam who recognised that they were damaged – resentful, ashamed, habituated to violence – and was prepared to manipulate them. It is not hard to see why fantasies about reinventing themselves as brothers in arms, defending their religion and their identity, appealed to them. But such fantasies were ultimately catastrophic, for themselves and total strangers, at a moment in French history when disaffected young men were being targeted by what Professor Olivier Roy has designated a modern species of death cult. Correctly identifying the nihilism of followers of organisations like ISIS, Roy offers an observation that applies very closely to the actions of Saïd and Chérif Kouachi: 'What fascinates is pure revolt, not the construction of a utopia. Violence is not a means. It is an end in itself. It is violence *devoid of a future*.' [My italics][10]

The fact that so many terrorists are suicidal has received less attention than it deserves, especially when you consider that it makes them much more dangerous than extremists who retain some hope of surviving; men who have chosen to carry out a suicide mission aren't going to be deterred by the prospect of being shot dead or blown to pieces. It's sometimes explained in terms of expectations of a better life in paradise, something which is mentioned on occasion by jihadists in advance of a terrorist attack, but that doesn't explain the fact that the same is true of so many mass shooters who *don't* have a religious motivation. Few mass murderers have any expectation of surviving, often ending a massacre by shooting themselves in the head if they haven't already been brought down by police bullets – what's known in the US as 'suicide by cop'. None of these men value their own lives, harbouring feelings of inadequacy and humiliation that develop over time into self-loathing.

Finding external scapegoats may make life tolerable for a while, allowing them to blame all their problems on a group of people identified as the enemy, with women and Jews being favourite targets. The Toulouse terrorist, Mohammed Merah, was openly anti-Semitic, murdering a teacher and three children at a Jewish school before dying in a shoot-out with the police, but the fact that he had previously made a failed attempt to hang himself in prison in 2008 is less well known – and is revealing about his state of mind. Because they kill so many people, this aspect of terrorism tends to be overlooked, even though it speaks volumes about the self-hatred of the perpetrators. Chérif Kouachi's self-destructive impulses were already evident in one of the documents discovered on his computer by the French police in 2010, entitled 'Operation Sacrifice', which outlined a terrorist attack very like the one the brothers would carry out five years later. It included this paragraph: 'A mujahideen forces his way into the enemy's base or else a zone where there is a group and fires at point-blank range *without having prepared an escape plan*. The goal is to kill as many of the enemy as possible. *The author will very likely die himself.*' [My italics][11]

The striking thing about this document is that Chérif – and most likely Saïd as well, given the symbiotic nature of their relationship – was already contemplating a suicide mission. The twin urges to kill and be killed existed long before the brothers heard that *Charlie Hebdo* had published cartoons lampooning the Prophet, suggesting that the contents of the newspaper merely provided a pretext to act on a rage that had needed an outlet for years. It also confirms that their amateurish flight from the newspaper office, when they gave away their location the following day by holding up a petrol station in a hijacked car, was no accident; they hadn't got an escape plan because they neither expected nor wanted to survive.

The bonds of family life, which might have acted as a restraint on other men, were not strong enough to deter them from a course of action that would end in their own deaths – as well as inflicting incalculable damage on their families. Saïd's wife Soumya was unable to work after being diagnosed with multiple sclerosis, leaving her financially dependent on him, and the couple had a three-year-old son. A year after the massacre, Soumya would issue a statement through her lawyer, expressing the immense bitterness she felt towards her husband for abandoning her and their son. But Saïd's experience of being a father didn't soften his behaviour towards Corinne Rey, a female cartoonist he encountered at the entrance to the *Charlie Hebdo* office, where she had arrived late for the editorial meeting after picking up her daughter from day care. Saïd and Chérif greeted her by her pen name, 'Coco', and threatened to shoot her and her child if she didn't key in the code they needed to get through the steel security door into the building.

Early that morning, Saïd had kissed Soumya goodbye at their flat in Reims, telling her he was going to visit Chérif in north-west Paris. He knew perfectly well that the next time she heard about her husband and brother-in-law it would be in connection with the country's worst terrorist attack in decades, yet there was nothing in his demeanour to suggest anything out of the ordinary. In a telling detail, survivors of the *Charlie Hebdo* massacre remembered that it was Saïd, always the quieter and more introverted of the two brothers, who did most of the killing.

When they shouted about avenging the Prophet, they were really talking about themselves, seeking vengeance for the anger and hurt they had been accumulating for decades. The argument that this type of terrifyingly destructive male rage is infantile in origin – that the psychological damage comes first and *enables* the ideology – is at the heart of this book. As we shall see in the next chapter, terrorist attacks like the *Charlie Hebdo* massacre are home grown, but not in the way that people usually mean when they use that phrase.

2

Everything You Need to Know About Domestic Violence

It's much more common – and more dangerous
– than you think

Few people realise how widespread domestic abuse is or how much police time it takes up. It accounts for almost *a third*[12] of violent crimes recorded by the police nationally but even the government acknowledges that this figure is a poor indicator of the real extent of abuse, which it describes as 'hidden'. You almost certainly know someone – a friend, relative or neighbour – who has been abused, but they're unlikely ever to show up in official statistics. Victims are afraid they won't be believed, afraid of breaking up the family and afraid, with good reason, of further violence from their husband or partner. They keep what's happening behind closed doors, often out of misplaced feelings of shame, and even those women who do finally get up the courage to report are assaulted on average *thirty-five times* before they dial 999 or walk into a police station.[13]

It's even harder for a woman from an ethnic minority community to tell the police about a violent husband, father or parent-in-law, especially if the victim has insecure immigration status. A voluntary organisation which offers specialist support to women from such communities in Wales lists some of the consequences of leaving an abusive household:

When a BAME woman leaves a violent home, she has made a devastating and often irreversible decision. She may have left the only family she knows in this country. There is a strong possibility that she and her children will be unable to return to her community or locality, due to threats, being dishonoured or stigmatisation.[14]

According to the Office for National Statistics, which carries out annual surveys of people's *experience* of crime, as opposed to what's recorded by the police, an estimated 1.9 million adults in England and Wales were victims of domestic abuse in the year ending March 2017. Just under two thirds of this figure (1.2 million) were women, but the ONS estimate of an additional 713,000 adult male victims gives a distorted impression of the proportion of female perpetrators. It is undeniable that some women abuse their partners and indeed their children, and we will encounter a particularly distressing example of the latter in chapter four of this book. When women *are* charged with attacking husbands or male partners – after killing a spouse, in the most extreme cases – it often emerges that they acted in self-defence after suffering years of beatings and sexual violence. But the fact remains that most abusers are men, and male victims of abuse include individuals who are in same-sex relationships. Not all victims are adults, of course, and every year there is a handful of cases in which a man murders his children to punish his partner for leaving him. Sometimes he kills the woman as well – such cases are known as family anni-hilation or familicide – and they result in murder prosecutions if the perpetrator hasn't committed suicide.

Even so, a large proportion of 999 calls relating to domestic abuse don't lead to a prosecution, as the ONS acknowledges:

> Approximately half of domestic abuse-related crimes that are recorded by the police do not result in an arrest and a large proportion have evidential difficulties in pro-ceeding with prosecution. Evidential difficulties often relate to the victim not supporting the prosecution. This reflects the challenges involved in investigating domestic abuse-related offences and demonstrates the importance of a robust evidence-led case being built for the victim.[15]

It isn't surprising that victims are reluctant to go through with the lengthy process of waiting for a criminal trial, given that some of them are still living in the same home as the abuser. The scope for intimidation is immense and women know perfectly well that they are at much higher risk than men of being killed; two women are killed each week by a current or former partner, according to the Home Office. The Counting Dead Women Project*, now the Femicide Census, lists 139 women killed by men in England, Wales and Northern Ireland in 2017; sixty-four (46 per cent) were killed by a current or former partner, eighty-two (59 per cent) died at home and ten women were killed by their sons. For the first time, the census collected data on 'over-killing', where the force used was much greater than that needed to kill the victim, and the results were shocking: it appeared in fifty-eight cases (42 per cent), including one in which a woman was stabbed 175 times and another where the victim was struck forty times with an axe.

These are unofficial figures but domestic abuse has a dramatic impact on British murder statistics, which show that fully *half* of female victims are killed by current or former partners, compared to only 3 per cent of male victims.[16] In London, there were twenty-four murder and manslaughter cases associated with domestic abuse in the year 2015–16 alone.[17] In 80 per cent of those cases, there was no previous warning in the two years

---

* Started by the feminist campaigner Karen Ingala Smith in 2012, it has now become the Femicide Census and is run by Ingala Smith in partnership with Women's Aid: www.womensaid.org.

before the fatal offence, confirming how little of even the most serious violence is ever reported to the police.

Tellingly, at the time of writing, murders of women *because* they're women don't count as a hate crime in this country. In October 2018, the government asked the Law Commission to consider whether misogyny should be added to a list of 'protected characteristics' which already includes race, religion, trans identity, sexual orientation and disability – a half-hearted acknowledgement that women are among the most frequent targets of hate crime. Not all feminists want to have misogyny added to the list, fearing that prosecutors would demand concrete evidence of hatred of women in cases of domestic and sexual violence, raising the bar for conviction even higher than it already is. But the fact remains that misogyny is at the heart of domestic abuse, with perpetrators using their female partners as scapegoats for all the disappointments and grievances in their lives. They dehumanise women, treating them as possessions instead of people, and the thing they fear most is being left – not just because of the rejection, but because of the loss of control.

The answer to 'Why doesn't she leave him?' may well be that she has nowhere else to go, but it's also because her husband or boyfriend has told her in graphic detail what he will do if he comes home and finds her gone. Some men openly threaten to kill their partners and children, while others hold the threat of suicide over their heads to stop them leaving; organisations that support abused women know that those who have recently separated have the highest rates of injury and death, compared to every other group of women.[18] It's why refuges need to invest so heavily in security, keeping their locations secret and restricting physical access to the building, yet the danger posed by the most extreme abusers is poorly understood by the general public. The police know better in London, at least: one senior officer, who has an unusually enlightened attitude to domestic violence, told me he warns his junior officers to treat call-outs to domestic incidents as homicide prevention.

So what do we know about the men responsible for most of this violence? At first sight, evidence about victims, from the government's survey of intimate partner abuse, among other sources, suggests that they come from deprived backgrounds; women with degrees or diplomas are significantly less likely to become victims of abuse than women who have only GCSEs or no qualifications.[19] According to the same survey, more than *three times* as many women in the lowest income bracket, defined as households with an income of less than £10,000 a year, experienced domestic abuse in the most recent year for which figures are available, compared to women in households earning more than £50,000.[20] A similar pattern is repeated up and down the country, so that women living in the 20 per cent most deprived areas of England are more likely to be victims of abuse than those in the 20 per cent most affluent areas.[21] In terms of recorded crime, the London boroughs with the highest levels of deprivation, measured in terms of people who are unemployed, unable to work or live on the minimum wage, also have the highest levels of domestic abuse – Croydon has much worse figures than the wealthy London borough of Richmond, for instance. It makes sense that overcrowded housing, strained finances and low self-esteem have an impact on behaviour; in a study of convicted terrorists in France, deprivation emerged as one of the most significant common denominators, with the subjects displaying poorer integration into the labour market, lower levels of education and more criminal convictions than the average French citizen.[22]

We also know that angry men are likely to self-medicate, using alcohol or drugs, and a significant number of victims of domestic abuse say that their abuser was using one or the other (17 per cent alcohol, 12 per cent drugs) at the time of an attack.[23] These figures are very likely an underestimate, given that women are understandably reluctant to implicate a dangerous partner in illicit drug use, even to an impartial researcher. But the idea that domestic abuse is linked to a deficient sense of masculine identity is reinforced by the nature of that drug use, which has been linked with anabolic steroids.[24] These are synthetic male hormones, taken to bulk up body mass, and overuse is associated with a hyper masculine appearance – bulging neck and arm muscles – as well as outbursts of aggression known colloquially as 'roid rage'. The connection between steroids and domestic abuse has been known about for years, but what has begun to emerge more recently is the fact that synthetic male hormones are the drug of choice for terrorists. The inquest into the deaths of the London Bridge perpetrators heard that they had high levels of the steroid dehydroepiandrosterone (DHEA) in their blood on the night of the attack, and the Westminster Bridge terrorist had been using steroids for years.

The problem, of course, is that an apparent statistical correlation between deprivation and domestic violence may be hiding abuse in wealthier households. An affluent woman with professional qualifications has more options than a mother of four children living in a council flat where the tenancy is in the name of the man who is abusing her. Wealthier women may choose to leave a controlling or violent partner without ever involving the police, skewing records of recorded abuse, and they may not feel like talking about it to anyone once they've put it behind them.

Whatever the truth of all this, however, one thing is clear: nothing, whether it is deprivation, substance abuse, mental illness or low expectations, excuses abusive behaviour. One of the things we should be most worried about is how often it *is* explained away or excused, as though violent men lack self-control and can't help themselves. The truth is that the cultural prohibitions on male violence aren't strong enough – and its eruptions don't stay neatly in one category, as we shall see time after time in this book.

A piece of research carried out by the VAWG team at the Mayor of London's Office for Policing and Crime examined a random sample of 500 individuals with repeat convictions for domestic abuse, drawn from data on the Police National Computer, to find out what else, if anything, they had convictions for. The results were eye-opening: violence 'features heavily' across the cohort and the men had an average of almost *seventeen* convictions apiece; three quarters had been convicted of violence against the person, 62 per cent had committed offences against property and the same proportion had convictions for offences against police officers, court officials or prison officers.[25] Normalisation of domestic abuse, in other words, is creating a pool of angry men with an unusually low threshold for other forms of violence.

Extreme domestic abuse is domestic terrorism

Domestic violence affects many more women than terrorist attacks. In 2017, which was a particularly bad year for bombing and vehicle attacks in England, the Femicide Census recorded twenty-one female fatalities at the hands of terrorists compared to sixty-four women who were killed by current or former partners. A marauding attack lasts a few moments or hours, until the perpetrator dies by his own hand or is killed by armed police, but domestic violence goes on for years and even decades. In its most extreme form, it is a kind of slow-motion terrorism, subjecting entire families to almost unimaginable levels of fear and anxiety – and sometimes ending in murder.

In July 2016, a man called Lance Hart lay in wait for his estranged wife, Claire, and her nineteen-year-old daughter,

Charlotte, as they emerged from a morning swim at a leisure centre in Spalding, Lincolnshire. The two women had left him five days earlier after suffering years of coercive control, a form of abuse that stops short of physical violence but restricts every aspect of the victims' lives. Hart, who was fifty-seven, controlled his wife's access to phones, insisted on taking the wages from her job, refused to give her access to the family bank account, accused her of being gay or having affairs, and kept her up all night while he got drunk and berated her. Even before Claire and Charlotte moved out, something they had planned months in advance, Hart had carried out Internet searches on men who murder their wives. As the two women emerged from the leisure centre, he shot both of them and then killed himself. Claire's sons, Luke and Ryan Hart, have since become campaigners against domestic violence, talking in detail about the kind of behaviour they endured while they were growing up. Luke's summary of Lance Hart's behaviour is succinct and devastating: 'Our father was a terrorist living within our own home; he had no cause but to frighten his family and to generate his own esteem from trampling and bullying us. For over a decade we had tried to leave on numerous occasions but he manipulated and threatened us on every occasion.'[26]

Luke Hart's testimony is a powerful rejoinder to the infuriating narrative that perpetrators of extreme domestic violence are kind, decent family men who simply 'snap' in a 'moment of madness'. They are not: these are men who terrorise their families and, if they are denied access to their primary victims, go on to find someone else. Because domestic abuse isn't taken sufficiently seriously in this country, there is nothing to stop a man convicted of seriously hurting a former partner leaving prison, moving to a different part of the country and starting the whole cycle over again. There *is* a domestic violence disclosure scheme, commonly known as Clare's Law, which provides a 'right to ask' the police about a new partner's previous convictions, but it isn't widely used and depends on individual police forces holding up-to-date information. Unlike convicted rapists and paedophiles, who have to sign the sex offenders register and tell the police each time they move to a new address, there is currently no register for men convicted of domestic abuse. This applies even if a man has been convicted of killing his wife or a former partner, a gap in the law which has led directly to the deaths of several women. The criminal careers of two British men, Theodore Johnson and Simon Mellors, speak volumes about the failure of the criminal justice system to recognise the risk that serial domestic abusers pose.

Theodore Johnson's murder conviction in January 2018 was greeted with shock and horror. It was a textbook punishment killing, motivated by jealousy and a thwarted sense of ownership. Furious that his ex-partner Angela Best, who was thirteen years younger than him, had begun a relationship with another man, sixty-four-year-old Johnson lured her to his home in north London where he hit her with a claw hammer and strangled her with a dressing-gown cord. Ms Best had no idea, when she first met Johnson several years earlier, that he had already killed *two* previous partners, a fact he concealed from her for several years.

Back in 1981, Johnson had used a similar degree of violence to kill his wife, Yvonne Johnson, hitting her with a vase before throwing her off the balcony of their ninth-floor flat in Wolverhampton. He was charged with murder but claimed at his trial that he had been provoked – and the jury believed him. Johnson was convicted on the lesser charge of manslaughter, served a much shorter sentence than he would have got after a murder conviction and, on his release from prison, moved to London where his criminal history wasn't known. He began a relationship with another woman, Yvonne Bennett, and they even had a child together – something that didn't stop him strangling her in 1993. This time, Johnson either knew the ropes or got good legal advice, agreeing to plead guilty to manslaughter to avoid another murder trial. He was sent to a secure hospital but applied for conditional release after four years, agreeing that he would tell the authorities if he formed a relationship with another woman. Johnson ignored the condition when he met Ms Best, and it was only when she found letters in his home that she discovered his dreadful history.

Johnson was violent and controlling, punching her in the face on at least one occasion, but he talked Ms Best into staying with him, perhaps because she was frightened of what he might do if she left. When she finally plucked up the courage to leave him in 2016, Johnson began stalking her, telling her that he loved her and threatening to take an overdose. He pleaded with

her to go to his flat, on the pretext of helping him with a passport application, and killed her when she arrived. The judge at
his murder trial described Johnson's criminal history as 'almost
unprecedented', a judgement which couldn't be further from
the truth. Mary Mason, CEO of the domestic-violence charity
Solace Women's Aid, got closer to the truth when she described
the case as 'misogyny in its worst form'.[27] Even then, her organisation had to appeal to three senior judges to get his prison
sentence, which the higher court agreed was unduly lenient,
increased from a minimum of twenty-six to thirty years.[28]

Violent men are often self-destructive as well as posing
a threat to other people, as we saw in the previous chapter.
Johnson appeared at his trial in a wheelchair after throwing
himself under a train shortly after he killed Ms Best; a fifty-
six-year-old convicted murderer called Simon Mellors hanged
himself in prison while he was awaiting trial for the murder of
his second victim, Janet Scott, fifty-one, in January 2018. When
she met Mellors, during a short separation from her husband
in 2017, Ms Scott didn't know that he had been released from
prison on licence after being convicted of the murder of his
estranged partner, Pearl Black, in 1999. The murder was particularly vicious: Mellors bludgeoned Ms Black with an iron
bar before strangling her. Her family objected to his release,
warning that he was quite capable of killing again, but their
apprehensions were ignored. When Ms Scott ended her brief
relationship with Mellors, he began stalking her, followed her
to work in Nottingham and threatened to kill both her and

her husband. Finally he stabbed her, chased her in his car and ran her down, killing her and injuring a traffic officer who had stopped to give her first aid. Between them, Mellors and Johnson killed *five* women in a series of brutal domestic homicides – and both were released by the criminal justice system to kill again.

If extreme domestic abuse shares features with terrorism, we should not be surprised by cases in which violence against intimate partners acts as a species of rehearsal for public acts of carnage. It explains how some men and even adolescent boys become desensitised to fear and anxiety, coming to think of them as a useful means of getting their own way. Misogyny sanctions a habit of mistreating people they're supposed to love, getting them used to observing and even enjoying the effects of pain. A small but significant number of these perpetrators persuade themselves (or they can be persuaded) that it would be legitimate to transfer their violence to the public sphere. Few recent cases illustrate the progression more vividly than that of a fifteen-year-old schoolboy from North Yorkshire, Thomas Wylie.

In the summer of 2018, Wylie appeared at Leeds Crown Court, charged with conspiracy to murder. He was accused alongside his friend, Alex Bolland, but Wylie was described as the ringleader in a plot to shoot teachers and blow up the school they attended in Northallerton. Both boys, who were only fourteen when they were arrested in 2017, hero-worshipped Eric Harris and Dylan Klebold, perpetrators of one of the most notorious school shootings in American history at Columbine High School in Colorado in 1999. Wylie carried out Internet searches on how to make nail bombs, boasting in his diary that he intended to commit 'one of the worst atrocities in British history'. Despite his youth, he was already a committed racist and right-wing extremist, telling the police that he wanted to kill people who were 'infecting the gene pool'.[29] But what most commentators missed was the key role of domestic abuse in the build-up to the plot, with some of the most disturbing evidence coming from Wylie's ex-girlfriend.

She was a vulnerable teenager, already self-harming, when they met via social media. Wylie targeted her deliberately, assuming the role of a caring friend who understood what she was going through, but it was actually a deeply controlling relationship; he insisted that she hand over all the passwords to her social media, texting her dozens of times if she failed to answer his phone calls. The abuse escalated when Wylie produced a scalpel and began carving his name into her back, pausing when she tried to distract him but finishing the job a few days later with a penknife. It's hard to think of a more graphic act of ownership, branding the girl like a slave, but it's also an example of an abuser practising his sadism on an intimate partner. Tragically, his victim broke down while she was giving evidence and talked about how much she missed him, suggesting that she had become habituated to abuse. Wylie was convicted of unlawful wounding as well as conspiracy to murder, and was sent to prison for twelve years, while his accomplice, Bolland, got ten years. The case aroused huge interest, but press reports focused on the Columbine angle, demonstrating how easy it is to miss the close connection between private and public violence.

The next generation

Just as the number of adults affected by domestic violence tends to be underestimated by the general public, the same is true of the proportion of children living in abusive households. According to Refuge, the charity that supports women and children escaping from violent relationships, *one fifth* of children in the UK have lived with an adult abuser; that figure includes an estimated 40,000 babies under the age of twelve months, a period when infant brains are developing rapidly and are highly vulnerable to stress. As well as witnessing violence against their mothers or older siblings, well over half of these children (62 per cent) will be directly harmed themselves.[30] The Children's Commissioner for England, Anne Longfield, has published some of the most up-to-date research on prevalence, estimating that 2.1 million children are growing up in families where there are serious risks and 825,000 of those are exposed to domestic violence.[31] (These figures don't include Scotland, Wales and Northern Ireland, but they do at least give some idea of the scale of the problem.) The impact on children used to be described as a 'cycle of violence' which turned a proportion of abused kids into violent adults, something identified in a report from the UN children's agency, UNICEF, back in 2006. It said:

> The single best predictor of children becoming either perpetrators or victims of domestic violence later in life is whether or not they grow up in a home where there is domestic violence. Studies from various countries support the findings that rates of abuse are higher among women whose husbands were abused as children or who saw their mothers being abused.
>
> Children who grow up with violence in the home learn early and powerful lessons about the use of violence in interpersonal relationships to dominate others, and might even be encouraged in doing so.[32]

UNICEF identified a range of behavioural problems in children exposed to domestic violence, including depression, suicidal tendencies, lack of empathy, aggressive behaviour and a greater risk of substance abuse. A more recent report from the same agency estimated that a third of children exposed to domestic violence would become aggressive themselves, while one in five 'acts out' (giving in to destructive impulses) or has difficulty making friendships.

It is more common these days to talk about a series of adverse experiences that affect children, and to argue that it is a combination of these ACEs – neglect, mental illness, sexual abuse, separation, divorce, substance abuse, loss of a family member through imprisonment or death, and domestic violence – that does the damage. Research carried out by the Welsh government found that adults who reported four or more ACEs in their background had a dramatic series of negative outcomes: they were fourteen times more likely to have been a victim of violence in the previous twelve months and fifteen times more likely to have committed it, as well as twenty times more likely to have been in prison at some point.[33] The Children's Commissioner talks about 100,000 children living with what she calls a 'toxic trio' of domestic violence, drug or alcohol misuse and mental illness, including 50,000 kids under the age of five and 8,300 babies under the age of one.[34] Her research suggests that another 160,000 children under the age of five live in a household where two of the three most toxic risk factors are present. Overall, the Commissioner's annual study of childhood vulnerability estimates that 1.6 million children in England are in effect 'invisible', receiving no support from the system that's supposed to help them.[35]

The sheer number of older children and adolescents who have grown up in toxic households has forced a major rethink by the authorities, including key elements of the criminal justice system. Experts have begun to talk about 'trauma-informed' approaches, which look at causes of risky and criminal behaviour as well as outcomes. Increasingly, the police are having to deal with a phenomenon called 'complex victimisation' where teenagers come to their attention as offenders but turn out to have been victims of crime themselves; a particularly distressing example involves underage girls arrested for criminal offences associated with gangs, such as hiding weapons or luring other girls into situations where they will be raped, who have often been sexually assaulted themselves at an earlier stage.

Dealing with these damaged children and teenagers takes up an increasing amount of police time and in 2017 the Metropolitan Police appointed its first head of safeguarding, Commander Richard Smith, who has extensive knowledge of gangs and knife crime in the capital.

'From the moment domestic abuse is happening, that's a risk factor,' he told me, pointing out that ACEs increase both the risk of health problems, often related to drug or alcohol abuse, *and* of ending up in custody. Smith believes that opportunities to intervene are being missed because outsiders don't spot what's going on in abusive families, even when children are sending distress signals. 'There is academic evidence that young children who experience abuse and exploitation will express what's happening to them several times before people notice it,' he added.

Smith insists that none of this is inevitable and the damage may be reduced by one of the protective factors I alluded to in chapter one, such as being taught by an inspirational teacher. More controversially, some professionals who work with damaged teenage boys argue for the need to find a healthy outlet for testosterone, such as joining a boxing club. But senior police officers understand that the fight/flight/freeze response, which is a natural human reaction to threatening situations, isn't much use to children who live with a violent parent.

'If you can't escape and freezing is to no purpose, you might decide to make friends with or be affectionate towards your abuser, just to survive,' Smith told me, referring to a mechanism – identification – which leads boys to side with a violent father as a means of survival. By the time these boys become teenagers, a proportion are already damaged and susceptible to predators of various sorts, whether they're gang members – the process Smith has seen on many occasions – or extremists. 'They may already be desensitised to violence, lacking in empathy and unable to manage impulses because of their age,' he said. 'They seek excitement and they're not able to think through consequences.' He believes that the effects of ACEs last much longer than most people realise, calling into question arbitrary distinctions in the way the criminal law approaches fifteen- and nineteen-year-olds: 'Children and young adults up to the age of twenty-five are at high risk of criminality and risky behaviour. They have high suicide rates and their impulse management is poor.' He adds that the threat of going to prison, even of losing their lives, has little impact on members of what he calls the 'gang cohort', who are able to keep up a delusion about their own immortality into their mid-twenties.

Everything Smith says about teenagers who get involved in gangs could equally be applied to young adults drawn into terrorist activities. Theories about a 'cycle of violence' depended in large part on observation but neuroscience has developed to a point where the impact of ACEs can be observed in brain scans. Infant nervous systems aren't fully formed and repeated surges of stress hormones appear to inhibit development, with some studies suggesting that parts of the brains of maltreated children are up to 6 per cent smaller.[36] One key study, published in 2011, highlights another difference which could be highly significant in terms of teenagers and adults who go on to become involved in violent extremism. The researchers used functional magnetic resonance imaging (fMRI) to show that two areas of the brain associated with the ability to detect threats, the anterior insula and amygdala, are as active in child victims of family violence as in the brains of soldiers exposed to combat.[37] They display what's called 'hypervigilance', resulting in a poor ability to assess risk *and* a tendency to overreact to perceived threats. The effects vary according to sex: girls who grow up in abusive households may lack the ability to judge the danger posed by a prospective partner, explaining why some women end up in relationships with a series of violent men. As for boys, it isn't difficult to see how hypervigilance might create another generation of abusers, responding angrily (and with their fists) to female partners who defy their wishes.

What has barely been considered until now, however, is how this character trait might interact with the efforts of terrorist organisations to radicalise young adults. It is clear that some individuals – most of them in their teens and twenties, the age group Richard Smith identifies as prone to risky behaviour – are unusually susceptible to approaches from extremists. In the last four or five years, a number of teenage girls from the UK and western Europe have been persuaded to go to Iraq or Syria by male members of ISIS they hadn't even met, responding to improbable offers of love, marriage and an idealised life in the caliphate; such behaviour makes more sense if it happens in the context of girls who have grown up with a limited capacity to understand risk and assess the intentions of predatory older men. At the same time, if we consider the effects on boys' brain development of living from infancy with a violent father, it should no longer come as a surprise if some of them develop into hypervigilant men who perceive threats round every corner. They are in effect programmed to be receptive to extremists, whether it's Salafist clerics telling them that Muslims are under attack and need to fight back or neo-Nazis spreading propaganda about the supposed threat from immigrants. This is precisely what happened to Saïd and Chérif Kouachi when they encountered a sequence of ill-intentioned father figures in Paris, each of them more than ready to exploit the humiliation and rage that were a legacy of their childhood.

In the world's current polarised state, it is becoming apparent that the effect of being exposed to several ACEs, including domestic violence, is even more dangerous than we thought. Not all abusive men bring up sons in their own violent image, but a significant proportion do. And some of those abused children, as we shall see in chapter four, will go on to become terrorists at home or travel abroad to join extremely dangerous organisations in Africa and the Middle East.

3

How Abusers Become Terrorists

This chapter examines some of the most horrific terrorist attacks of recent years, covering events in the UK, France, Spain, the US and Australia. The men who commit these atrocities are often treated as though they emerge from nowhere, suddenly engaging in a single, inexplicable act of violence that couldn't have been predicted or stopped. What these life stories show, on the contrary, is a long history of abuse and assaults on women – wives, girlfriends, sisters – which demonstrates how deeply misogyny is implicated in the formation of men we think of primarily as terrorists. They show perpetrators practising and evolving in private, becoming desensitised to violence and its effects long before they move their violence on to the public stage. What begins at home doesn't always stay there – and here are some of the dreadful consequences.

Westminster Bridge

At 2.40 p.m. on the afternoon of Wednesday, 22 March 2017, a man called Khalid Masood carried out the first successful attack in an English city since the 7/7 bombings almost twelve years earlier. Masood drove at speed across Westminster Bridge, mounting the pavement and brutally mowing down pedestrians. Leaving a trail of casualties, he crashed his rented SUV into the railings surrounding the Palace of Westminster, where he leapt from the vehicle armed with a pair of kitchen knives. Running through the gates into New Palace Yard, where MPs and ministers emerge into the open from Westminster Hall, he confronted two unarmed police officers and began stabbing one of them. PC Keith Palmer, a popular officer who was well known to people who worked in Parliament, collapsed to the ground and Masood advanced further into the yard, looking, according to one witness, for more police officers to attack.

He was confronted by two armed close-protection officers who happened to emerge from Parliament at that moment, waiting for their 'principal', a Cabinet minister, to follow them out of the building. '[Masood] was carrying two large knives and I could see clearly that they were covered in blood,' one of the officers said at his inquest, eighteen months after the attack. 'I shouted at him to drop the knife or drop the knives, I don't recollect the precise words. It had no effect. He continued to move towards me. He was going to kill me.'[38] Masood, it would later turn out, had high levels of steroids in his blood and the officer, realising he was not going to stop, shot him three times.

Meanwhile a government minister and former army officer, Tobias Ellwood, had rushed to PC Palmer's side and was trying to use his knowledge of first aid in a desperate attempt to keep him alive. Paramedics arrived and took over from Ellwood, working on the victim and the perpetrator just yards apart, but were unable to save either man. The entire attack had lasted just eighty-two seconds and left five people dead, in addition to Masood, and twenty-nine injured. In an area crowded with tourists, the fatalities included an American visitor, who died at the scene, and a young Romanian woman who was thrown from the bridge into the Thames by the impact of Masood's SUV. She was rescued from the river by boat but died later in hospital from her injuries, as did a retired window cleaner from south London. The final victim was a PA from a nearby sixth-form college, who was hit by Masood's vehicle as she crossed the bridge to collect her daughters from school.

Naturally, there was intense interest in the identity of the attacker. Despite an opportunistic claim from ISIS, it appeared that Masood was a so-called 'lone wolf' terrorist and a number of people arrested in the aftermath of the attack were released without charge. Masood turned out to be well known to the police, although not on suspicion of terrorist offences, and he had also been on the radar of MI5 for a period without ever becoming a major suspect. He is one of the most consistently violent men in this cohort of recent terrorists, accumulating a daunting criminal record over twenty years before apparently undergoing a change of heart and settling down to a quiet life with his second wife and the younger of his four children. At the age of fifty-two, he was much older than most terrorist suspects and the fact that he had been known by at least three different names at different times in his life caused some confusion. He was born Adrian Russell Elms – Elms was his mother's surname – in south-east London in 1964 but was known as Adrian Ajao, using his stepfather's surname, until he legally changed his name to Masood in 2005 following his conversion to Islam. He acquired seven convictions between 1983 and 2003 – most of them committed in Sussex, where he lived at the time – for a series of violent offences including criminal damage, possession of an offensive weapon, threatening behaviour, actual bodily harm, assault on police and unlawful wounding.

At his inquest in September 2018, eighteen months after the attack, it emerged that his own mother regarded him as an angry person and had worried, when he was a young man, that he would kill someone during a fight. An old police intelligence report observed that he 'seems to have a violent temper which he has demonstrated in a number of crimes [. . .] each of them seeming to be progressively worse'.[39] Masood had a liking for knives, the weapons he used on PC Palmer, and he had a terrifying propensity for cutting people's faces although he was not averse to using his fists or a baton on occasion. Sections of his criminal record were read out at his inquest, including an incident in July 2000 when he slashed a man's face with a knife as he was thrown out of a pub; he was sentenced to two years and is believed to have become interested in Islam, and begun his conversion, while he was in one of three different prisons where he served time.

More violence followed his release from jail: there were incidents when he smashed a glass over a man's head, cut a second man's face with a knife, coshed someone during a robbery and broke another man's collarbone with a baton. Witnesses were often too frightened of Masood to give evidence against him – he was accused of intimidation on more than one occasion – and his own mother told his inquest she compared him to the Incredible Hulk after he made a furious scene over a chicken dinner. In May 2003, in one of the most horrific incidents in his criminal career, Masood plunged a carving knife through the nose of a man who accused him of being an undercover police officer, forcing it down into his mouth until the blade broke. Masood was charged with attempted murder and wounding with intent but was acquitted, reportedly to the amazement of the trial judge, after claiming he had acted in self-defence.

In December 2003 he was released from prison, where he had been remanded in the run-up to the trial, and appeared to turn over a new leaf. In what looked like a complete break with the past, there were no more arrests and not a single further conviction in the thirteen years before Masood achieved notoriety as one of this country's most remorseless terrorists. What *didn't* appear on his lengthy criminal record, although it certainly existed and continued long after his reinvention, was his extensive history of domestic abuse.

Masood's first long-term relationship was with a woman called Jane Harvey, with whom he lived in a village in Sussex, and the couple had two daughters. Masood was arrested several times during the relationship, usually after he had been drinking, and his mother told his inquest that Ms Harvey called to ask for help on several occasions when Masood walked into the house and started shouting. The relationship broke down after he was sent to prison for the first time in 2000, amid what was described at the inquest as 'ongoing domestic abuse'. By then, Masood already had a history of attacking women, dating back to an incident in 1998 when he lost his temper with someone he was trying to chat up; Masood accused the woman of disliking him because he was black and punched her in the face although the victim insisted, with what sounds like good reason, that it was his attitude to women that she didn't like. The attack doesn't seem to have resulted in a prosecution but at some point over the next couple of years, Masood *was* convicted and fined for causing actual bodily harm to a girlfriend – the sole occasion on which his abuse of women came to public notice.

In 2004, shortly after his acquittal on the attempted murder charge, Masood moved to Crawley, which was becoming a meeting place for some of the more notorious members of the Islamist organisation, al-Muhajiroun, which was later banned by the government under legislation outlawing the 'glorification' of terrorism. Unsurprisingly, in the light of his history, Masood was attracted by Wahhabism, the puritan-ical and deeply misogynistic form of Islam followed in Saudi Arabia, an absolute monarchy where public exhibitions of vio-lence, floggings and executions are sanctioned by the regime. It evidently suited Masood, who taught English in Saudi Arabia in 2005–6 and again in 2008–9. By April 2004, even before his first trip to the kingdom, he was already beginning to gravitate towards extremists in the UK, coming to the attention of MI5 when a telephone number associated with him appeared in the contacts of a man suspected of planning a bombing – almost certainly Waheed Mahmood, who lived in Crawley and was one of five men found guilty in 2007 of conspiracy in the so-called 'fertiliser' bomb plot. MI5's files don't suggest that Masood had a direct connection with that plot but he turned up on the periphery of various spin-off investigations between 2004 and 2009, when the security service stepped up its interest in him because of his trips to Saudi Arabia. Masood became an active 'subject of interest' (SOI) in February 2010 but intelligence suggesting he might be helping men travel to Pakistan for terrorist training with AQ was 'low level, uncorroborated' and later judged to be incorrect. A couple of weeks later, his status was downgraded by MI5 from someone who posed a threat to national security to that of someone who *might* pose a threat, and a review in December 2010 recommended that his case should be closed.

It didn't happen immediately but even when he was no

longer officially of interest to the security service, Masood turned up as a contact of a number of active SOIs, including individuals linked to ALM in Luton and Crawley; one of them was Abdul Waheed Majeed, who is believed to have carried out the first suicide attack by a British national in Syria when he drove a lorry packed with explosives into a prison in Aleppo in 2014. There isn't any intelligence to suggest that Masood was a member of ALM himself but the method he used on Westminster Bridge – an assault with a vehicle, followed by a lethal assault with knives – was almost identical to the attack on Fusilier Lee Rigby four years earlier, which *was* carried out by ALM supporters. Masood certainly expressed views shared by members of ALM, including approval of the 9/11 terrorist attacks in the US, but his lengthy preparations for the Westminster Bridge attack were not picked up by the security services.

In the previous year, 2016, he told his family he was planning to go and work abroad while he was secretly researching terrorist attacks, knives and types of vehicles online; in the couple of weeks before the attack, he bought two knives at a Tesco in Birmingham, browsed YouTube for videos related to terrorism and sent himself an email headed 'Retaliation'. David Anderson's review of the attack concluded that Masood hadn't given MI5 reason to reopen its investigation into him:

Subsequent searches of various media devices belonging to him concluded that he appeared to advocate a conservative, Saudi-influenced, Salafist interpretation of Islam, but noted that his relatively small digital collection did not contain much of the standard jihadi content that is normally found in investigations involving Islamist-inspired terrorists.[40]

We know from Anderson's review of the 2017 attacks that a history of domestic violence wasn't on the radar of MI5 or counterterrorism police in this period. To all intents and purposes, Masood looked like a man who had some suspicious connections but had successfully renounced his violent past. Nothing could have been further from the truth: what Masood actually did was *privatise* his aggressive behaviour, hiding it behind closed doors and very effectively avoiding further convictions.

In September 2004, he married a Muslim woman of Pakistani heritage, Farzana Malik, whom he had known for only a few weeks. Ms Malik was more than a decade younger than Masood and he immediately embarked on a regime which would now be recognised as an extreme form of coercive control; he gave her five strict 'rules' to follow, including restrictions on what she watched on TV and when she was allowed to meet non-Muslims. Unsurprisingly, the marriage didn't last, with Ms Malik deciding within months that she had to escape from Masood. 'He was very violent towards her, controlling in every aspect of her life – what she wore, where she went, everything,' a relative confirmed after the Westminster Bridge attack. 'He was a psychopath and I mean that in the very medical definition of the word. He came from a nice family, had everything, but there was something very wrong with him.' Ms Malik was so terrified of her husband that she fled to the other end of the country, taking all her possessions in a single suitcase.[41] Masood didn't give up, tracking her down at her new address, but she insisted on a divorce.

The episode offers a very different picture of Masood from the apparently reformed character that emerges from his criminal record, and his second marriage – to a woman from a Gambian background whom he met in 2006 – would be characterised by shouting, threats and coercive control. Giving evidence at the separate inquest into her husband's victims, also in September 2018, Rohey Hydara said Masood was 'controlling and angry' and described how he threatened her with divorce when she refused to stop wearing trousers. They also argued over his use of steroids, which Masood began taking in 2009, prompting another threat of divorce. 'He would get very bad when he was on steroids,' Ms Hydara said, adding that she secretly taped some of Masood's furious diatribes. On one of the tapes, which was played in court, Masood could be heard ranting at Ms Hydara for refusing to see 'any good' in ISIS and failing to obey him.[42] The couple appear to have been living separately at the time of the Westminster Bridge attack.

Masood's conversion from recidivist criminal to apparently devout husband and father was always improbable, especially to anyone familiar with the trajectory of domestic abuse. Perpetrators rarely give up, finding justifications for their behaviour towards women and children – Masood is said to have 'effectively abducted' one of his daughters when she was sixteen in a failed attempt to force her to convert to Islam – and finding new victims when one escapes. He is not just a man whose violence jumped categories, although it did, but one who decided, with an unusual degree of calculation, to restrict it to the private sphere in a successful attempt to avoid further collisions with the criminal justice system. 'They'll say I'm a terrorist, I'm not,'[43] he told his mother in a cryptic remark six days before the attack – but he had already been a domestic terrorist for most of his adult life. The knowledge that Masood had privatised his aggressive tendencies – and that they were now specifically tied to a puritanical form of Islam – might have helped the security service to come to a different assessment of how dangerous he was. If Khalid Masood looked like a reformed character, it was only because he got smarter as he got older – and learned to conceal his violence in the private sphere.

Finsbury Park

On Sunday, 18 June 2017, just over two weeks after the London Bridge terrorist attack, a forty-seven-year-old man called Darren Osborne drove to London from Wales in a rented van. He spent part of the day driving round London, intending to attack an annual march in support of the Palestinians, but was unable to get close enough because of security arrangements. Frustrated and angry, he looked for an alternative target and ended up just after midnight in Finsbury Park, north London, where worshippers were leaving the local mosque after Ramadan prayers. A frail older man, fifty-one-year-old Makram Ali, had collapsed and a crowd was gathering on the pavement. Seeing a group of people in Muslim dress, Osborne decided he had found what he was looking for. What happened next was described by the judge at Osborne's murder trial, Mrs Justice Cheema-Grubb, who addressed him directly. She said:

> You accelerated the van towards them intending to kill as many people as you could. The fact that traffic was stopped at lights just before the side road where the crowd was and you had to cross a bus lane meant that you were able to reach no more than about sixteen miles an hour before you struck them.
>
> Over twelve innocent members of the public were struck and injured. Makram Ali, who was lying on the ground, was run over with the tyre-marks left on his torso. He died immediately because internally his heart was severed from vital vessels.[44]

Another victim, Hamid al-Faiq, was trapped under the van, suffering complex fractures. The judge praised an imam, Mohammed Mahmoud, who intervened to stop Osborne being attacked by a crowd who had dragged him from his van. 'I said he should answer for his crime in court, like he is doing now,' Mr Mahmoud said in evidence, 'not in a court in the streets.'

Although the attack was clearly a copycat of the Westminster and London Bridge incidents, Osborne was charged with murder and attempted murder rather than terrorist offences. He was said to have shown no interest in Islam or Muslims until three weeks before the Finsbury Park attack when he watched a BBC drama-documentary, *Three Girls*, which told the story of underage girls who had been groomed and raped by a gang of British-Pakistani men in Rochdale. Family and neighbours in Wales said that Osborne began railing against Muslims after he saw the documentary, going on the Internet and searching for right-wing and anti-Muslim organisations. He joined Twitter just before the London Bridge attack and started following accounts linked to right-wing organisations, including Britain First, which was founded by former members of the British National Party. On the evening before he drove to London, Osborne was thrown out of a pub in Pentwyn, near Cardiff, after claiming to be a soldier – a common fantasy among extremists, sadly – and shouting that he was 'going to kill all Muslims'.[45] At his trial, he came up with a flimsy story that the van used in the attack had been driven by a man called Dave, but the jury found him guilty on both counts. The judge used her powers to give him an aggravated sentence of forty-three years, in recognition of the fact that his offences were related to terrorism.

Most commentators focused on how quickly Osborne had been radicalised, along with the fact that he had done it by searching online for extremists who fuelled his rage. They missed two things: Osborne had long been an angry white man, a domestic abuser with a lengthy record of violent crime, and his transformation into a right-wing terrorist coincided with a crisis in his domestic life.

Born in Singapore to a father who was in the RAF, Osborne spent his formative years in the seaside town of Weston-super-Mare, where he became known locally as a troublemaker – a 'serious fighter who got off on violence and liked to be the centre of attention',[46] according to a friend who remembered him from those days. At his trial, the judge summarised his appalling history, telling him bluntly:

You have not worked for ten years. You abused alcohol. You were described as a loner and nondescript. You took medication for depression. You have 102 criminal convictions acquired from your youth onwards. They include offences of public disorder and violence, including assaulting the police. You have experienced youth custody and sentences of imprisonment. Over the years you have been given help to reform with probation and community rehabilitation orders, but your response was often to breach those orders. Your record reflects a belligerent and violent character.[47]

Osborne's previous convictions included one for grievous bodily harm in 2005, handed down after he attacked a drinking friend with a bicycle lock, breaking his jaw. During his trial for that offence at Swindon Crown Court, it emerged that he already had four convictions for actual bodily harm – the most recent, in 2003, for domestic violence against his female partner.[48] It wasn't the first time Osborne had attacked a woman: back in the 1990s, when he was living in Weston-super-Mare, he grabbed an eighteen-year-old woman by the throat, pinning her against the wall in the pub where she worked. He and his partner were eventually forced to leave the town, spending a short time in Swindon where Osborne was convicted of GBH before they ended up in Cardiff. In the decade before the Finsbury Park attack, he made little attempt to change his behaviour, impressing one neighbour as 'quite a shouty person, always shouting at his wife and kids'.[49]

It all came to a head in the weeks leading up to the attack, when his partner seems to have decided she'd had enough; neighbours heard fierce rows and Osborne moved out of the house, although he was allowed back to see his four children. He was effectively homeless, telling a local barber he had slept in a tent in the woods for a couple of weeks, while neighbours also spotted his tent in the garden of the family home. The night before he drove to London, police officers who were called out following reports of a man sleeping in a van discovered Osborne, drunk and insensible, inside the vehicle he would use in his attempt to kill total strangers twenty-four hours later.

After decades of heavy drinking, fighting and domestic abuse, Osborne's life had finally come apart. In a familiar pattern, he was suicidal and didn't expect to survive the attack, leaving a note in the van which said he expected to be shot dead by the police. 'Suicide by cop' didn't work out as he planned, any more than an attempt to kill himself by throwing himself into a river a few weeks earlier. Osborne's family believe he was mentally ill, a view challenged by people who see it as an excuse for right-wing terrorism, but years of heavy drinking had almost certainly had negative effects on his brain. His former partner believed he felt 'worthless', suggesting a degree of self-hatred common among angry men, and a chance viewing of a TV documentary provided him with a scapegoat.

Osborne's trajectory – short-tempered thug, domestic abuser, terrorist – closely resembles that of Khalid Masood, despite the fact that they were supposedly inspired by radically opposed ideologies. Right-wing extremists and Islamist-inspired terrorists are more alike than they would ever admit, reluctant to restrain their violent impulses and practising on the women they claim to love.

Pulse Nightclub, Orlando

In the early hours of Sunday, 12 June 2016, a twenty-nine-year-old man called Omar Mateen walked into a gay nightclub in Orlando, a city in central Florida about two hours' drive from his home in Fort Pierce. Mateen was a security guard, used to carrying a gun, and he was armed with two deadly weapons, a SIG Sauer MCX rifle and a Glock semi-automatic pistol, which he had purchased legally in the days before the attack. He was able to buy guns despite the fact that he'd expressed sympathy with Islamists, going back years, falsely claiming after the 9/11 suicide attacks that Osama bin Laden was his uncle and had taught him how to use an AK-47. He had been investigated by the FBI in 2013, after boasting to colleagues that he had family connections to AQ, and again in 2014 when a man who attended the same mosque in Florida, Moner Mohammad Abu-Salha, went to Syria and blew himself up in a suicide attack on behalf of the al-Nusra Front.

Inside the crowded nightclub, Mateen opened fire, causing panic and a desperate rush to find places to hide. Terrified clubbers hid in bathrooms, sending frantic text messages to their loved ones as Mateen roamed the building, picking off the survivors. When the police arrived he took hostages, holding out for the best part of three hours and making a series of calls from his mobile phone. In one of them, to the 911 emergency number, he described himself as a soldier, pledged allegiance to the leader of ISIS, Abu Bakr al-Baghdadi, and several jihadists, including Abu-Salha and the Boston marathon bombers, Tamerlan and Dzhokhar Tsarnaev. Mateen was eventually killed in a shoot-out with the police at around five a.m., leaving forty-nine people dead and fifty-three wounded. It was the deadliest mass shooting by a single perpetrator – and the worst attack on LGBT people – in American history, with a death toll that would be surpassed only by the massacre at a Las Vegas music festival fifteen months later.

In the aftermath of the attack, Mateen's motives came under intense scrutiny. His father, a self-aggrandizing figure in the Afghan exile community with well-known homophobic views, denied that Mateen was an Islamist and suggested he was disgusted by seeing gay couples display affection in front of his young son. People who had known Mateen as a teenager and younger man, on the other hand, suggested that he was himself gay or bisexual. The FBI later said they had found no evidence that Mateen used gay dating sites, but it isn't unusual for individuals to register under a different name. His ex-wife, Sitora Yusufiy, said in an interview with *Time* magazine that she wondered during their brief marriage whether her husband was hiding his sexual orientation from his parents. 'In his family structure, homosexuality was really not tolerated,' she said, after the attack. 'And one of the directions of his life was to be the perfect son.'[50] If Mateen was trying to conceal his sexuality from his family, and indeed himself, he would constantly have had to struggle with the gap between reality and the macho image he wanted to project – and the women in his home would have been easy targets for his anger. His trajectory follows a familiar pattern, finally settling on LGBT people as scapegoats in much the same way that Osborne targeted Muslims and the Kouachi brothers made themselves feel important by despising non-Muslims and Jews.

What seems clear is that Mateen was a fantasist, claiming connections to terrorist organisations in a misguided attempt to impress school friends and work colleagues. His problems stretched back to his childhood in Florida when he was bullied because of his weight, responding by becoming a bully himself and narrowly escaping prosecution when he attacked another pupil. His teachers thought he needed help but his father wouldn't listen, treating female teachers in particular with a marked lack of respect. The angry teenager turned to bodybuilding, changing his appearance dramatically as he worked out obsessively and took steroids. His search for a new identity included a legal change of name in 2006, just before his twentieth birthday when – for reasons that remain unclear – he added the surname Mateen to his original name, Omar Mir Seddique. He was desperate to join the police, an ambition that was thwarted when he was thrown out of a training academy after threatening to bring a gun on to the campus. He had a work history of minimum-wage jobs in shops and fast-food outlets before he got a job – which came with a gun and the uniform he longed for – with the security company G4S, in 2007.

Mateen's history is an almost parodic version of a man undergoing a masculinity crisis, bulking himself up with steroids and claiming non-existent links to terrorist organisations while trying to get jobs in law enforcement. It would not be surprising if he wrestled with his sexual orientation and tried to mask it through a parade of heterosexual relationships, inevitably adding domestic violence to his record of impulsive and disturbed behaviour. He met both of his wives online, marrying women from distant parts of the US – New Jersey, in Ms Yusufiy's case, while his second wife, Noor Salman, was living on the other side of the country in California when they first connected.

Mateen married Ms Yusufiy, an estate agent whose family was originally from Uzbekistan, in April 2009, and it didn't take long for her to realise that her new husband was an abuser. In a classic pattern of controlling behaviour, he confiscated her salary and refused to allow her contact with her family; he was physically violent as well, once trying to choke her because she hadn't finished the laundry. After four months of abuse, Ms Yusufiy's parents realised what was going on, came down from New Jersey and had to physically wrest her from their son-in-law's arms as he tried to stop her leaving him.

Mateen's second wife was not so lucky. Noor Salman, whose Palestinian parents came to the US from the West Bank, was divorced after an arranged marriage that did not work out. She met Mateen on a dating site called Arab Lounge and married him at a mosque in Rodeo, California, in 2011. In another pattern familiar to experts on domestic abuse, he started attacking her when she became pregnant, punching her and threatening to hit her harder if she told anyone. After interviewing Ms Salman, the *New York Times* described the abuse she suffered in detail:

When [Mateen] became angry, he would start biting his lips and clenching his fists. In public, he also had a code word he used if she was doing something he didn't like. He would call her 'shar'. That was short for *sharmuta* – slut or whore in Arabic.

He would also pull her hair, something she has since learned he also did to his first wife. He choked her and threatened to kill her. He never said he was sorry. 'He had no remorse,' she said.[51]

In this second marriage, unlike the first, Mateen had a hold over his wife: they had a child together and he threatened that he would get custody of their son if she tried to leave. On the night of the attack, she was in bed when he sent her a text message in the early hours, asking whether she knew what had happened. Hours later, the FBI came to the house and revealed that her husband was the perpetrator of the nightclub attack.

From the outset, the FBI suspected that Ms Salman knew about Mateen's plans in advance. Very unusually, in a development which exposes a failure by the American criminal justice system to understand how women are controlled by their abusers, she was charged with being her husband's accomplice and spent four months in jail awaiting trial. The prosecution case rested on a confession she signed following an interview which lasted almost twelve hours, carried out directly after the attack, when she was in a state of shock and wasn't represented by a lawyer. The FBI agents failed to tape the interview and a key prosecution claim, that Ms Salman had gone on a reconnaissance mission to the nightclub a few days before the attack, fell apart when phone records showed neither she nor her husband was anywhere near it on the day in question. She was tried on charges of obstruction of justice and of aiding and abetting her husband, a man she accused of beating, raping and imprisoning her in their home. In March 2018, not quite two years after the massacre, Ms Salman was acquitted on both counts. Like other widows of terrorists, she has been left with the task of bringing up her son on her own – and one day having to tell him why he doesn't have a father. While Mateen is rightly reviled as the perpetrator of the worst homophobic attack in American history, he was also a domestic tyrant who tried to compensate for gnawing feelings of inadequacy by beating up women in his own home.

London Bridge

Khuram Butt, ringleader of the London Bridge terrorist cell, stands out among the perpetrators of the 2017 terrorist attacks as the only one who was under active investigation by MI5. He was a known associate of extremists, including members of ALM, and featured in a Channel 4 documentary, *The Jihadists Next Door*, in which he was shown posing with an ISIS flag. He had been an active SOI for two years at the time of the attack, assessed by MI5 as posing a medium risk 'due to his strong intent but weak capability'.[52] For a time, Butt seemed more interested in travelling to Syria to fight with ISIS than staging an attack in the UK, but in the second half of 2016 he re-engaged with his extremist friends in ALM and was arrested in October that year on suspicion of bank fraud. Over the next few months, MI5 appears to have been unsure how much risk he posed, downgrading his status as a suspect but deciding in May 2017, the month before the attack, that further investigation was needed.

Butt was born in Pakistan and came to the UK at the age of eight when his family claimed political asylum, eventually being granted indefinite leave to remain in 2004. He went to school in Forest Gate, east London, and became a British citizen when he was fifteen. Between 2012 and 2015, he worked as an office manager for a subsidiary of the American fast-food chain, KFC, marrying the sister of a friend in 2013 and living with her in a flat in Barking, east London. Butt acquired two cautions for minor offences but he didn't have a criminal record and little is known about his marriage, apart from the fact that his wife always appeared fully veiled in public. He made no attempt to conceal his misogyny, expressing the view that women shouldn't be allowed to work outside the home; in the summer of 2016, when he was employed for four months as a trainee customer-services assistant by Transport for London – Butt worked at Canada Water, Southwark and Westminster stations before his performance was deemed unsatisfactory and his contract was terminated – he complained to a colleague about having to deal with 'scantily clad' women. His disapproval extended to women in cycling gear, according to a neighbour in Barking who recalled the 'sinister' looks he gave her when she rode past on her bike, while another female neighbour said she contacted the police after Butt approached her children in a local park and tried to convert them to Islam.

But it is his attitude to his own family which is most revealing, reflecting the emotional detachment we have already seen in other aspiring terrorists: his wife was pregnant with their first child when he announced his intention to abandon her and travel to Syria to fight for ISIS, a plan which was frustrated only when his passport was taken by family members, preventing him from leaving the country. His wife gave birth to a son in October 2014, and their second child, a daughter, was born in May 2017 – something that didn't alter Butt's plans one jot.

Around ten p.m. on the evening of Saturday, 3 June, Butt and two accomplices drove a hired van on to the pavement at London Bridge, killing two people. Wearing fake suicide vests, they jumped from the van armed with large knives and savagely beat a British Transport Police officer who bravely confronted them on his own. They then ran into Borough Market, where restaurants and bars were packed with people enjoying a perfect June evening, slashing at passers-by as bar staff tried frantically to barricade the doors. Butt and his accomplices managed to murder six more people before armed police arrived and shot them dead, the final seconds of their lives captured on shaky videos by horrified witnesses. His daughter was only days old at the time and his wife, now a widow, had barely had time to recover from the birth before images of her husband's dead body, lying on the ground, wearing the shirt of his favourite football team, Arsenal, under his dummy suicide vest, began to circulate on the Internet and news sites.

David Anderson's report points out that Butt employed 'strong operational security' and that much remains unknown about both his 'mindset' and the planning that went into the attack. We know a great deal less about him than the other men who committed terrorist attacks in the UK in 2017 and it is impossible to say definitively whether he was a domestic abuser, although his frank misogyny and callous attitude towards his wife and children suggest he was a controlling husband at the very least. Like other terrorists in this book, his view of father-hood was instrumental – serving a psychological need for a time but readily abandoned when another, more pressing aim intruded. It is a telling commentary on the patriarchal model of family life, in which the father's status and his absolute right to make life-and-death decisions matter more than human relationships.

The elder of Butt's two accomplices, a thirty-year-old Moroccan called Rachid Redouane, *did* have a record of domestic abuse, as well as being known to the police as a failed asylum seeker. MI5 believe that the two men met at the Ummah Fitness Centre in Ilford, east London, probably in December 2016, six months before the attack and not long after Redouane finally managed to enter the country legally. He had been trying to get into the UK since 2009, when he falsely claimed to be a Libyan asylum seeker, was turned down and absconded. Redouane was arrested in Scotland in 2012, still using a fake Libyan name, as he tried to board a boat to Northern Ireland; deportations to Libya had been suspended because of the civil war so Redouane was released and returned to Morocco, where he met an Irish woman called Charisse O'Leary. They married in 2012 but had to live apart until 2015 when Redouane was granted an Irish visa and travelled to Dublin to join his wife. Ms O'Leary sponsored his application for an EEA residence card and the couple moved to London while she was pregnant with their first child; there is no doubt that the marriage was genuine on her part but the speed with which they moved to London, fulfilling Redouane's long-held ambition to live in the UK, has raised suspicions about his motives for marrying an Irish citizen. The couple's daughter, Amina, was seventeen months old at the time of the attack but by then Ms O'Leary had left Redouane, complaining about a sustained campaign of violent abuse which began when she refused to convert to Islam. According to the *Mirror*, which interviewed friends of Ms O'Leary after the terrorist attack:

> [Redouane] would attack her in the street if she answered him back and he tried to ban her from eating anything other than halal food.

> A friend of Charisse, 38, said: 'We'd try to arrange to meet for coffee but she would call and say, "I can't".

'It would either be, "he's slapped me in the middle of the street today" or "he's kicked me" or "he will not let me out of the house".

'He did not want her to drink or smoke – he wanted her to wear a hijab, he wanted a traditional Muslim wife, and Charisse was not that.'[53]

Redouane's attempts to control his wife soon extended to his daughter, on whom he tried to impose bizarre restrictions: he announced that the toddler could not go to dancing classes and must not watch TV 'in case it made her gay'.[54] Ms O'Leary left him in January 2017, restricting contact to occasions when he came to see Amina. She had just arrived back from a barbecue when he turned up at around seven p.m. on the evening of 3 June, cradling his daughter and kissing her. Three hours later, Redouane took part in the London Bridge attack, leaving Amina without a father. Four days later, Ms O'Leary issued a statement unequivocally condemning what her husband had done. She said: 'Rachid and I had been separated for six months. We have a beautiful young daughter, that for the last six months has been our only bond and reason for contact. My thoughts and efforts now are with trying to bring up my daughter with the knowledge that some day I will have to try and explain to her why her father did what he did.'[55]

As well as killing and injuring more than fifty complete strangers, Redouane and Butt left three children without fathers. It isn't something that's much discussed after a terrorist attack, when public sympathy naturally lies with the people who have been injured and killed, but deliberately exposing young children to the loss of a father in such terrible circumstances should in itself be regarded an extreme form of domestic abuse. Such a callous disregard for family life, love and responsibility doesn't happen overnight, speaking volumes about what these men were like to live with *before* they moved their hatred and rage on to the public stage.

Birstall, West Yorkshire

On Thursday, 16 June 2016, a week before the EU referendum, the Labour MP Jo Cox was attacked in Birstall, a small town in her constituency, about eight miles south-west of Leeds. Cox was forty-one and had only been elected at the previous year's general election, but she had already made a name for herself as a passionate supporter of humanitarian causes, including the White Helmets civil defence organisation in Syria. Thomas Mair, a fifty-two-year-old unemployed gardener, shot Ms Cox in the head, stabbed her and began to walk away, returning to shoot her twice more and stab her again when he realised she was still alive. In all, Ms Cox suffered fifteen stab wounds and died in the back of an ambulance, despite frantic efforts to save her.

As he carried out the assault, Mair shouted slogans such as

'Britain first', making it clear from the outset that the murder was a right-wing terrorist attack. When police went to his home on the nearby Fieldhead council estate after arresting him, they discovered a mass of material about the Nazis, white supremacism and the apartheid regime in South Africa. When he was asked to confirm his name in court, a couple of days later, Mair blurted out: 'My name is death to traitors, freedom for Britain.' He had a history of mental illness but a psychiatrist found no evidence that his mind was impaired when he attacked the MP. Five months later, in November 2016, he was convicted of murder, grievous bodily harm against a retired miner who tried to help Ms Cox, and possession of a firearm and a knife. The judge, Mr Justice Wilkie, imposed a whole-life sentence, telling Mair that the only circumstances in which he could ever be released were on humanitarian grounds, in order to allow him to die at home.

Mair's history left no doubt that he was a committed extremist. His contacts with right-wing organisations were extensive and he was said to have admired David Copeland, the neo-Nazi who carried out the Soho pub bombing. He lived alone, had never married, didn't have a girlfriend and gave every indication of being a lonely obsessive. At first sight, that differentiates him from the other terrorists in this chapter, most of whom had abusive relationships with one or more women. At Mair's trial, however, the judge made a revealing observation as he described the meticulous planning that went into the assassination. He described how Mair had carried out research on Ms Cox over a period of weeks and had looked for information about how to modify the stolen gun he used to kill her. Then he said: 'You informed yourself about previous murders of civil rights workers and a past assassination of a serving MP. You contemplated the aftermath, researching lying-in-state arrangements. *You even researched matricide*, knowing that Jo Cox was the mother of young children.' [My italics][56]

While most of the judge's sentencing remarks were admirable, he misunderstood both the meaning of the word 'matricide' and its significance in this case. Matricide *isn't* the murder of someone who just happens to be a mother; it's a form of extreme domestic violence in which a son or (more rarely) a daughter kills their own mother. Such cases are rare but the search terms Mair used confirm that he was thinking about the murder of his *own* mother, Mary, not his eventual victim, Ms Cox. One of his searches was for 'son kills mother for miscegenation',[57] a highly offensive and rarely-used word for people from different ethnic groups having children together – and an unambiguous reference to Mair's mother.

Mair was born in Kilmarnock, East Ayrshire, but his parents split up and he moved with Mary to Yorkshire, where she began a relationship with a man called Reginald St Louis who had come to the UK from the Caribbean. The couple lived in Batley and had a mixed-race son, Mair's half-brother Duane, when he was ten years old. They married five years later, when Mair was fifteen, but by then he had gone to live with his grandmother in Birstall, in the house which was still his home at the time of Ms Cox's murder. His mother and stepfather split up and Mary married again, changing her second name to Goodall, and she insisted, after the assassination, that Mair had always been a kind and thoughtful son. His Internet searches tell a different story about his feelings towards her: in the days before he killed Ms Cox, Mair read the details of a real case of matricide in Japan, where a son killed his mother after she gave birth to a mixed-race child. The parallels with his own family history are obvious, suggesting that Mair was not only racist but nurtured a deep-seated grievance against his own mother – to the point of fantasising about killing her – for giving birth to his mixed-race brother.

Some reports of his trial suggested that he had gone as far as plotting to murder Mary Goodall, but it's clear that his feelings towards her were complex and conflicted. It seems more likely that he displaced his rage on to another target, a woman who was well known locally, easily recognisable when she came to Birstall and who represented all the liberal values that he hated. That doesn't mean the murder wasn't political: it was clearly an assassination, carried out in the highly charged atmosphere of the referendum campaign, and Mair deserves to be remembered, if at all, as a right-wing terrorist. But the origins of public violence are often more complex than they appear at first sight, and it seems likely that Mair's misogyny had been festering for years before it finally burst into lethal effect on the streets of West Yorkshire.

Boston Marathon

The Tsarnaev brothers, Tamerlan and Dzhokhar, arrived in the US from a troubled part of the world. Their father, Anzor, was from Chechnya, a mostly Muslim republic which fought two savage wars for independence from Russia in the 1990s and early 2000s, leaving the capital, Grozny, in ruins. Their mother, Zubeidat, was originally from Dagestan, on the Caspian Sea, but the family made a restless journey around the North Caucasus, trying to escape the effects of conflict and poverty. Tamerlan Tsarnaev was born in Kalmykia, part of the Russian Federation, while his younger brother and two sisters were born in Kyrgyzstan. It was not an easy family history to overcome but Anzor had ambitions for his sons, naming the elder after a nomadic Muslim warrior, Tamerlane or Timur, and the younger after the Chechen separatist leader, Dzhokhar Dudayev, who was killed in a Russian missile strike a couple of years after his birth. Anzor would later claim that he lost his government job and was beaten up and tortured during a purge of Chechens in Kyrgyzstan, prompting him to claim asylum for himself, his wife and his younger son during a trip to the US in 2002. His medical records, which were produced during Dzhokhar's terrorism trial in 2015, confirmed that he had extensive mental problems, including PTSD, panic attacks, insomnia, psychosis, memory problems and hallucinations.

The Tsarnaevs settled in Cambridge, Massachusetts, home to

Harvard University and one of the most liberal cities in the US, where eight-year-old Dzhokhar thrived in his new school and soon began to learn English. Tamerlan, who joined the family with his sisters a year later, was a different story; he was sixteen when he arrived in the US, never lost his strong Russian accent and claimed to have no American friends. Dzhokhar nevertheless idolised his older brother, especially when he seemed to have found a glamorous role in his adopted country. The boys' father, Anzor, had been an amateur boxer back home in the North Caucasus and Tamerlan followed in his footsteps, becoming something of a local celebrity – he was heavyweight champion of New England two years running. But he was already displaying signs of a toxic form of masculinity, arriving for boxing matches in a silver Mercedes he'd borrowed from his father's used-car business and wearing tight leather trousers, a look that was later described in an unflattering posthumous profile as 'small-time Russian pimp'.[58] He had already had a run-in with the police over domestic abuse, having been arrested for beating up his then girlfriend, Nadine Ascencao. The attack happened in a car, in full view of passers-by, as she recalled: 'He literally grabbed my jaw and he was telling me "you are not going to wear this, do you understand what I'm saying" and he kept pushing my head until I hit the car and it hurt and that made me really upset and he just slapped me across the face.'[59]

When the police arrived, Tamerlan admitted slapping Ms Ascencao and was charged with domestic assault and battery, a disastrous turn of events for a young man who intended to apply for American citizenship. Tamerlan needed an American passport to fulfil his ambition to be selected for the US Olympic boxing team, something that would have been jeopardised by a conviction for domestic abuse. He had a lucky escape when Ms Ascencao, like many women who have suffered violence at the hands of a man who is supposed to care about them, decided not to press charges. But Tamerlan was too headstrong to change his behaviour, getting a reputation among his cousins as a man who abused women. Boxing is sometimes regarded as a safe outlet for young men who have problems with aggression, as we saw in the previous chapter, but it evidently didn't work for Tamerlan. At home, he adopted the role of enforcer, beating up an American boy who went out with one of his sisters, apparently with his father's approval. In the end, such displays of aggression were self-defeating, bringing his boxing career to an abrupt halt: in the early stages of a competition in 2010, he couldn't resist taunting a rival fighter in his dressing room, annoying the man's trainer so much that he tipped off the boxing authorities that Tamerlan, who still had a Russian passport, wasn't eligible to compete. It was a devastating blow, although entirely self-inflicted, and appears to have been a decisive factor in his accelerating disillusionment with the US.

Blocked from the Olympic career he dreamed of, and with his ability to get an American passport in serious doubt, Tamerlan began looking for a new identity in radical Islam. His mother, Zubeidat, was moving in the same direction, abandoning the high heels and fashionable clothes she usually wore and starting to wear the hijab. She and her elder son became 9/11 conspiracy theorists and Tamerlan began downloading issues of *Inspire*, an online magazine published by AQAP, the terrorist organisation based in Yemen which provided military training to one of the *Charlie Hebdo* attackers. The first edition of *Inspire* described how to make home-made bombs in pressure cookers, the weapon Tamerlan and Dzhokhar Tsarnaev would use for their own terrorist attack in 2013.

Their mother's growing attachment to a strict version of Islam was symptomatic of wider tensions in the family. Anzor disapproved of her new religious affiliations, which caused marital rows, and his own health was deteriorating. In 2009, in the latest episode of a family history characterised by brushes with violence, Anzor got into a vicious brawl in a restaurant in Boston, which left him with a fractured skull and brain damage. His marriage fell apart, he could no longer work and in 2011 he took two big steps, getting a divorce and returning to Dagestan. He was followed a year later by his ex-wife, who skipped bail after being arrested on shoplifting charges, leaving their sons to depend ever more closely on each other.[60] The couple's daughters remained in the US where they would both go on to have unhappy histories: Alina Tsarnaeva's arranged marriage at the age of sixteen lasted for little more than a year and in 2014 she appeared in court, accused of making a bomb threat against the mother of her boyfriend's child, a charge she denied. Her sister Bella also had a failed marriage and was arrested in New Jersey on marijuana charges, after which she entered a pre-trial prevention programme.

Tamerlan was married by now, to an American woman he had been seeing secretly during his relationship with Ms Ascencao, but his habit of abusing women was ingrained. Katherine Russell came from a middle-class family in Rhode Island and her college flatmate, who got to know Tamerlan when the couple began seeing each other, remembered him as 'emotionally abusive' from the start. He was jealous, punching a man who said something he didn't like to Ms Russell, and he once played a cruel trick on her, pretending he'd infected her with AIDS after they'd had sex. The flatmate moved out, unable to stomach Tamerlan's behaviour, and under his influence Ms Russell underwent a dramatic transformation; she converted to Islam, changed her first name to Karima, started wearing the hijab and dropped out of college when the couple married in 2010. They soon had a daughter but becoming a father didn't stop Tamerlan following his own parents to Dagestan, where he briefly entertained a fantasy about joining a local jihadist group. Relatives talked him out of it and he returned to the US where, now aged twenty-six, he lived on state benefits and his wife's modest earnings as a care assistant, read jihadist material on the Internet and got into rows at the local mosque.

His younger brother, Dzhokhar, wasn't doing much better; at the age of nineteen, he was a struggling student at the University of Massachusetts, switching between courses, getting into debt and following in his elder brother's footsteps by tweeting conspiracy theories about 9/11. Life hadn't worked out as the brothers had hoped when their parents left the North Caucasus: the family was now dispersed, neither brother looked to the future with much optimism and Tamerlan had a violent, explosive temper. Concluding that the US was to blame for all his problems, Tamerlan decided to mount an attack on the country he had come to hate, and drew his adoring younger sibling into the plot. It's striking that, when they discussed a terrorist attack, the brothers – one of whom had been frustrated in his ambition to become an Olympic boxer – chose a target that symbolised the American enthusiasm for fitness and healthy living.

On 15 April 2013, a pleasant Monday afternoon in Boston, hundreds of runners were approaching the finishing line in the city's annual marathon when two home-made bombs exploded. This was not a suicide bombing: the devices had been constructed inside pressure cookers, concealed in backpacks and planted along the route of the race, with the aim of doing maximum damage to participants and spectators – but only after the perpetrators had moved to a safe distance. Three people were killed, including an eight-year-old boy, and at least 264 were injured, with sixteen people losing limbs.

Three days later, when the FBI identified Tamerlan and Dzhokhar Tsarnaev as their chief suspects, the brothers went on the run, shooting a police officer and hijacking an SUV. Just after midnight on Friday, 19 April, they were recognised and got into an exchange of fire with the police, creating a scene of carnage: both brothers were injured and Dzhokhar panicked, crushing Tamerlan under the wheels of the SUV as he tried to escape. Dzhokhar managed to get away, leaving behind Tamerlan, who was badly hurt but fought with paramedics who tried to save his life; he died shortly after arriving at hospital. A huge search for Dzhokhar ended when he was found, seriously injured, hiding underneath the covers of a boat in a garden in Watertown, Massachusetts. He was arrested and charged with thirty offences, including four counts of murder and a rare charge of conspiring to use a weapon of mass destruction resulting in death.

At his trial, Dzhokhar's lawyers didn't deny his part in the bombing but claimed it was the habitually violent elder brother, Tamerlan, who masterminded the attack. We have already seen that pairs of brothers feature strongly in recent jihadist attacks and it makes sense that the idea for the bombing originated with the petulant, self-aggrandising Tamerlan, but the bombing is also an example of how violence becomes normalised in families. The fact that Tamerlan abused women wasn't a secret, within the family or outside it, and it illustrates once again how dangerous it is to allow such men to avoid convictions.

In April 2015, two years after the bombing, the jury found Dzhokhar Tsarnaev guilty on all charges. He was sentenced to death by lethal injection, becoming the youngest person on death row in the US, where he remains at the time of writing.

Lindt café siege, Sydney

Shortly before ten a.m. on Monday, 15 December 2014, ten customers were drinking coffee and hot chocolate in the Lindt café in Martin Place, Sydney, where eight staff were employed in the run-up to Christmas. A fifty-year-old Iranian man calling himself Man Haron Monis, who had arrived in the café more than an hour earlier and ordered black tea and a piece of cheesecake, asked one of the staff if he could move to a table nearer to the rear of the café. He then went to the toilet before demanding to speak to the manager, Tori Johnson, whom he ordered to lock the café doors. Monis had brought a shotgun with him in a gym bag and he told Mr Johnson to make an emergency call, instructing him to say that everyone in the café had been taken hostage 'by an Islamic State operative armed with a gun and explosives'. Monis also claimed, without foundation, that three bombs had been planted by 'other brothers' at different locations in Sydney.[61]

During the siege that followed, Monis forced hostages to stand in front of the windows with their arms above their heads, ordered one of the women to hold up a black flag with white letters where it could be seen by TV cameras, offered to release a hostage in exchange for an ISIS flag and demanded a public debate with the prime minister. Monis wasn't able to keep an eye on all the people in the café and on Monday afternoon two of them escaped from the front door, while a third got out via a fire exit. Around ninety minutes later, two female employees escaped, but the siege dragged on through the evening and into the early hours of the next day.

Just after two a.m. on Tuesday morning, police and security services heard Monis fire a single shot at a third group of escapees, who fled unhurt from the building. Shortly afterwards he forced Mr Johnson to kneel on the floor with his hands on his head, firing a second shot high into one of the café walls. Another of the hostages managed to escape at this point, leaving only six inside the café with Monis, who was clearly losing control of events. At twelve minutes past two, he shot Mr Johnson in the head and a decision was taken to storm the café. Monis was killed along with one of the remaining hostages, a barrister called Katrina Dawson who died when a police bullet ricocheted and struck her. As well as the deaths of Mr Johnson and Ms Dawson, three hostages were injured in the rescue attempt. Notes found on Monis's body suggested that, unlike most of the terrorists who feature in this book, he had planned for the possibility that he would survive the attack; he was carrying a handwritten list of Muslim prisoners, complete with their custody numbers, whom 'he could contact if he ended up in jail'.[62]

In the days after the attack, it emerged that Monis was a conman with a staggering history of domestic and sexual violence. It was astonishing, in fact, that he was still a free man; only two months earlier, he had been charged with thirty-seven new sex offences in addition to three counts of indecent and sexual assault which had already been filed against him. But even that wasn't the extent of his involvement with the criminal justice system; just over a year before the siege, on 12 December 2013, he had appeared in court charged with being an accessory to the murder of his second ex-wife. The crime was horrific: the woman's body was found in the stairwell of his apartment block in Sydney where she had been stabbed eighteen times, doused with petrol and set on fire. The officer in charge of the murder investigation was so concerned when Monis was granted bail that she wanted the prosecuting authorities to apply to the Supreme Court for a review of the decision – but the official report of the inquest into the deaths at the Lindt café found that the police didn't make the necessary application.

Ten months later, when officers could have arrested Monis on the new sex charges, they merely served him with a notice requiring him to appear in court on 10 October 2014 – a decision described with some under-statement as a 'mistake' by the official report.[63] It observed that this error increased Monis's chances of once again being granted bail, despite the number and gravity of the offences he was facing. The report concluded that 'the prosecutor should have applied for Monis to be remanded in custody in relation to the sex offences and for his bail on the murder-related charges to be reviewed'.

The sex charges arose from a 'spiritual healing' business which was no more than a cover for repeated sex attacks. Monis advertised the business in newspapers, appealing to female migrants from Pacific islands where there is a widespread belief in magic. 'Is the time running out on you and are you still single?' one of his flyers asked. 'Do you want to clean the evil spirit and improve your spiritual life?'[64] Monis claimed to be an 'Expert of Relationship' [*sic*] and offered to cure the women's health problems through massage. His seven victims, who did not know each other, told pretty much the same story: Monis informed them they were under a spell or a curse, asked them to take off their clothes and began 'painting' their naked bodies with a wet brush before assaulting them. When a client tried to resist, 'he would tell her that sexual energy was the only way to cure her problem, or threaten to harm her with his magic powers if she refused the treatment'.[65]

One 'client' went to the police in 2004 after Monis told her she had cervical cancer, claimed he needed to destroy the 'evil' inhabiting her body and raped her.[66] It is hard for any woman to report a sex attack but the circumstances were stacked against his victims, who not only belonged to a disadvantaged ethnic group but would have had to admit to sceptical police officers that they believed in magic. Like many sexual predators, Monis was canny about the women he targeted, and he wasn't charged in 2004 – a failure of the criminal justice system which allowed him to go on assaulting women, and secretly videoing his sessions with them, until the police finally realised the extent of his attacks *eight years later*. By then, he was already plotting to murder his second and by now ex-wife.

Monis had arrived in Australia from Iran on a business visa in 1996, leaving behind his first wife and children after allegedly stealing money from a travel agency he worked for. The Iranians always maintained that Monis, whose original name was Mohammed Manteghi, was a fraudster and a crook but he claimed asylum in Australia, claiming that he belonged to a persecuted sect in Iran and was in danger from the government. The Australian security services investigated Monis and didn't like what they saw, concluding in 1999 that he might pose a threat to national security, but a year later they changed their minds. He was granted a protection visa in 2000 and became an Australian citizen in 2004.

Over the next few years, he changed his name several times, calling himself Michael Mavros, Man Monis and even Sheikh Haron. He had an extensive history with the security services, offering tip-offs about terrorist attacks that came to nothing, but also displaying views so extreme that they prompted more than forty calls to the government's national security helpline. He made a series of extremist videos, calling on Muslims to attack the then US President, Barack Obama, and was convicted of sending offensive letters to the families of Australian soldiers who had been killed in combat in the Middle East. Whether Monis was a committed supporter of ISIS, a fantasist or mentally ill has been the subject of fierce debate, and the diagnoses are not mutually exclusive. In the ten years before the siege, he saw numerous doctors and psychologists 'in connection with what can be broadly termed mental health problems' but 'no firm or reliable diagnosis was reached'[67]. What seems beyond question is that it took far too long for the police to recognise

Monis's history of violence against women, despite the fact that it was calculated, systematic and extreme.

Monis's second wife was a Fijian-Australian woman whom he met through the 'healing' business and he subjected her to years of domestic abuse, controlling every aspect of her behaviour and insisting that she wear the hijab. The couple had two children before they eventually divorced and the woman, who can't be named for legal reasons, reported Monis to the police in 2011, alleging that he had threatened to shoot her unless he was allowed greater access to his children. She was stabbed to death in April 2013 and Monis's then girlfriend, a Greek-Australian hairdresser called Amirah Droudis, was charged with the murder. Monis had made sure to provide himself with an alibi for the time in question, even staging a car crash outside a police station, and he was furious when he was charged as an accessory. He died in the Lindt café siege before he could stand trial but his story had a horrific (and telling) coda almost two years later.

In November 2016, Amirah Droudis was convicted of the 'frenzied' murder of Monis's ex-wife.[68] During her trial, it became clear that Droudis *had* carried out the murder on Monis's instructions after being subjected to a catalogue of violent abuse which placed her under his control. He had persuaded her to convert to Islam and change her first name from Anastasia to Amirah, repeatedly beating her up until she 'uncritically adopted and espoused Monis's vile beliefs'. In 2008 and 2009, when Monis was making his 'extreme and offensive' videos attacking Western leaders, Droudis appeared on camera wearing a niqab and praised Osama bin Laden. She also described the Bali bombers as martyrs and was an eager accomplice in Monis's campaign against the families of veterans. When he became involved in a custody dispute with his ex-wife, he first of all tried to organise a 'hit' by members of a biker gang, intending to get custody of their two children and bring them to live with himself and Droudis. The bikers didn't take him seriously and Monis decided to enlist Droudis instead, telling her to disguise herself in a niqab and lie in wait for his ex-wife at an apartment block in western Sydney. 'Monis planned the murder of his former wife, although he seemingly was not prepared to carry out the killing himself,' the judge said at Droudis's trial. Rightly observing that his role in the killing didn't reduce her culpability, he sentenced her to a minimum of thirty-three years in prison.

Few people would quarrel with the judge's description of Monis as 'evil' but it is troubling that this disturbed and violent man remained free to abuse women for so long. When he finally faced retribution, the prospect of spending years in prison was intolerable to his narcissism and he staged a violent diversion, acting out a fantasy of being a soldier in one of the world's most sadistic terrorist organisations. Monis is not the only perpetrator in this book who resorted to terrorism at a moment of personal crisis, revealing an aspect of toxic masculinity – a lethal tendency to lash out when cornered by their own behaviour – that hasn't received anything like sufficient attention. Neither an acrimonious divorce nor criminal charges cause men to become terrorists but they should be regarded as warning signs of possible escalation, especially if the individuals concerned have previously expressed sympathy for extremist organisations.

At the same time, the fact that Monis was released on bail speaks volumes about the failure of the criminal justice system to recognise the danger posed by men with histories of extreme violence against women. Monis was facing dozens of serious charges, which would almost certainly have resulted in a lengthy prison sentence, yet he was allowed to walk out of a courtroom on at least two occasions. Had he been remanded in custody, the siege in the Lindt café would never have happened, his ex-wife's family and the women he raped might have got justice – and the lives of two complete strangers would have been saved.

Barcelona and Cambrils

On Wednesday, 16 August 2017, a small house blew up in Alcanar, a coastal town in north-east Spain. Two men died inside the building, which turned out to be a bomb factory containing hand grenades, detonators and more than 200 kilograms of explosives. The next day, a twenty-two-year-old man drove a hired van into pedestrians on Las Ramblas, the most famous and crowded street in Barcelona, killing thirteen people and injuring another 130, including a German woman who died later in hospital. The driver then went on the run, hijacking a car and murdering the driver before he was cornered in a field several days later and shot dead by police. But that wasn't the full extent of this bizarre series of incidents: eight hours after the Barcelona attack, in the early hours of Friday, 18 August, a car drove at speed into pedestrians in the seaside town of Cambrils, around seventy miles south of Barcelona. Five men jumped out, wearing fake suicide vests, and started attacking passers-by with knives and an axe. One woman was killed and several people injured before the attackers were shot dead by armed police.

It soon became clear that both attacks were a panicked reaction to the explosion in Alcanar, which killed a forty-four-year-old man called Abdelbaki Essati – leader of an Islamist gang, self-styled imam and a convicted drug trafficker. The Alcanar blast, which was an accident, put an end to the gang's ambitious plans to stage terrorist attacks on well-known sites in Barcelona, including the church of La Sagrada Familia and FC Barcelona's Camp Nou stadium. Instead, the surviving members of the gang decided to improvise, using makeshift weapons – vans, cars and knives – in place of the ordnance they had lost in the blast. Most of the perpetrators were young Spanish-Moroccans, some of them still only teenagers, who had grown up together and gone to the same school in Ripoll, a town on the edge of the Pyrenees; in what is now a familiar pattern, they included four sets of brothers. Few of the suspects were previously known to the police and there is still a dearth of information about them and their relationships, with one exception.

At twenty-eight, Driss Oukabir was more than a decade older than the youngest men in the gang and, when his passport was found in the van used in the attack on Las Ramblas, it was initially assumed that he was the driver who escaped after the attack. Oukabir denied having anything to do with the Ramblas atrocity, claiming that his documents had been stolen and used to hire the van without his knowledge, but then his younger brother Moussa, seventeen, was identified as one of the men shot dead in Cambrils. Driss Oukabir, who already had convictions for driving while drunk and violence, was charged with belonging to a terrorist organisation, terrorism-related murder and possession of explosives.

In addition to his convictions, he had been arrested on two other occasions, on suspicion of aggravated robbery and rape, spending a month in prison in Figueres before the rape case was dropped due to insufficient evidence. He was also a habitual domestic abuser, something that emerged during a trial which took place while he was on remand in Madrid in 2018.[69] Only a month before the terrorist attacks, two women saw him assault his girlfriend in their block of flats in Ripoll, grabbing her by the hair and dragging her down the stairs – one of a series of similar incidents the witnesses were able to describe in detail. Their account was confirmed by two police officers who were called on the same night to the couple's apartment, where they found Oukabir's girlfriend sobbing and pleading for him to be taken away.

It isn't clear whether he had been charged with assault at the time of the terrorist attacks, but he was certainly facing a prison sentence if a prosecution went ahead. In the event, his trial for assault took place in jail, seven months after the Barcelona and Cambrils atrocities. Oukabir was convicted of domestic abuse and sentenced to six months in prison, to be served in addition to any sentence handed down in the terrorism case, which is still being investigated at the time of writing.

New York and New Jersey

Between 17 and 19 September 2016, several home-made bombs were left at a series of locations in New York and New Jersey. Fortunately, the would-be bomber was incompetent: one device exploded on the route of a charity race in New Jersey, but the track wasn't being used at the time and no one was injured. A second bomb exploded in the Chelsea district of Manhattan, injuring thirty-one people, while another device planted nearby failed to detonate. Back in New Jersey, a homeless man narrowly escaped death when he picked up a backpack containing a pipe bomb, which had been left by the same bomber in a railway station; the device didn't go off but a second bomb planted in the station exploded when a robot tried to defuse it.

The perpetrator had followed the same bomb-making instructions as Tamerlan and Dzhokhar Tsarnaev, published in the AQAP magazine *Inspire*, and he even left a note with one of the Manhattan devices that mentioned the Boston Marathon bombings. He also managed to leave behind his fingerprints, which were on record after the police were called to incidents of domestic violence – demonstrating how a previous arrest for abusing family members can be used to help a terrorist investigation. The suspect was quickly identified as a twenty-eight-year-old Afghan-American, Ahmad Khan Rahimi, who had arrived in the US in 2000. His large family lived in Elizabeth, New Jersey, fifteen miles from New York, where they ran a fried-chicken restaurant. Married, with a small son, Rahimi was in the midst of a bitter quarrel with an ex-girlfriend and had been arrested both for breaking a restraining order and for attacking members of his own family. The police named him as a suspect in the bombings and warned the public to report any sightings, saying he might be armed and dangerous.

As the hunt for Rahimi got under way, a bar owner in New Jersey spotted a man sleeping in a doorway. He called the police, who immediately recognised him as the suspect in the bombings. Rahimi woke up, pulled out a gun and shot one of the officers in the stomach before firing at a second policeman, who was sitting in a patrol car. Neither of the officers was seriously hurt and they returned fire, hitting Rahimi seven times during a protracted shoot-out. He was eventually arrested and rushed to hospital, where he survived after emergency surgery. On 20 September, he was charged with eight offences, including use of weapons of mass destruction and bombing a place used by the public. Just over a year later, after a two-week trial, Rahimi was found guilty on all charges and sentenced to life imprisonment without parole.

After his arrest, police found a bloodstained notebook in which he had made notes about the Yemeni-American hate preacher Anwar al-Awlaki, the Tsarnaev brothers and a senior figure in ISIS, but no evidence that he was in direct contact with jihadist groups – something that comes up time after time in cases where individuals appear to have been self-radicalised. What is evident, however, is that Rahimi's transformation into a terrorist followed a very similar pattern to that of Man Monis and Driss Oukabir, coinciding with messy events in his private life – principally a long-running battle with the mother of his daughter, who was originally from the Dominican Republic.

The couple met at school in New Jersey and their daughter was born in 2007, while Rahimi was in his final year, but the relationship was opposed by his father, who wanted him to marry a cousin in Afghanistan. Rahimi defied his family, moving in with his girlfriend's family and working in their shop for a time, but she eventually broke off the relationship. Rahimi returned to his parents' home, where he lived above the restaurant, and his father encouraged him to make several trips to Afghanistan and Pakistan. In 2011, Rahimi went through with an arranged marriage in Quetta and attended a religious seminary closely associated with the Taliban. Over the next three years, he spent long periods in Pakistan and Afghanistan, appearing to have become much more religious on his return to his parents' home in New Jersey. His wife gave birth to a son in 2014 but by then Rahimi was increasingly at odds with his family, especially his father, who later claimed he was so worried about his son's interest in jihadist preachers that he tried to contact the FBI in August 2014.

While it is often difficult to establish the truth of such claims and whether they were taken seriously by the authorities, what is not contested is that Rahimi was becoming unstable and violent. That same month, he physically attacked his mother and sister, and stabbed one of his brothers in the leg when he tried to intervene. The family went to the police, who arrested Rahimi and charged him with aggravated assault and unlawful possession of a weapon. While he was being held in jail, his ex-girlfriend went to court, claiming that Rahimi was involved in terrorist activity and was unfit to look after their daughter; she was awarded full custody of the child. The criminal charges were eventually dropped, at the request of his family according to some reports, but the following year his ex-girlfriend went to court again, suing Rahimi for more than $2,000 in unpaid child support.

The impact of all this on an angry man from a patriarchal family, who was increasingly inclined towards conservative religious ideas, is not difficult to imagine. Rahimi decided to buy a firearm – and despite growing evidence that he was prone to lashing out, there was nothing to stop him. In June 2016, he passed the necessary background checks and bought a Glock 9 mm handgun, the weapon he later used against the police officers who were trying to arrest him in connection with the bombings. Had Rahimi been tried and convicted on domestic-abuse charges in 2014, he wouldn't have been allowed to buy a firearm – further evidence, if any were needed, that the failure to prosecute violence against family members is likely to have serious and unforeseen consequences.

Promenade des Anglais, Nice

On warm summer evenings, tourists and local people mingle on the Promenade des Anglais in Nice, with the sea on one side and bars, restaurants and hotels on the other. The road was particularly busy on Thursday, 14 July 2016, Bastille Day, which was marked by a fireworks display towards the end of the evening. Just as the fireworks finished, a thirty-one-year-old man, Mohamed Lahouaiej-Bouhlel, turned a heavy hired lorry on to the promenade, which had been partly closed to traffic for the festivities. He drove on to the pavement, knocking down and crushing pedestrians, before returning to the road and forcing the lorry through barriers erected at the beginning of the traffic-free section. Lahouaiej-Bouhlel tried to steer the lorry back on to the pavement, intending to kill and injure as many people as possible, but his rampage was slowed by the actions of passers-by, who tried desperately to stop him. One man threw his scooter under the wheels of the lorry, jumped up to grab the door of the cab and was driven back by Lahouaiej-Bouhlel, who clubbed him with the butt of a gun. He then fired shots at the police, who chased the truck and tried to shoot out the tyres, until it came to a halt only five minutes after the rampage started. Lahouaiej-Bouhlel was shot dead by the police, leaving eighty-five people dead – another died later in hospital – and 458 injured.

As usual, ISIS was quick to claim Lahouaiej-Bouhlel as one of its followers, but he turned out to be a hedonistic man whose abrupt turn towards religious extremism was in contrast to the way he conducted most of his life. He was born in Tunisia, where his family lived not far from the tourist resort of Sousse, and relatives said he had suffered a series of mental breakdowns before he moved to France. At one point, his family sent him to a psychiatrist, who assessed him as a narcissist who was obsessed by his appearance; Lahouaiej-Bouhlel liked to think he resembled the Hollywood actor, George Clooney, and he would later become a bodybuilder, posing for photos that showed off his arm muscles and torso. By the time of the attack, he was well known to the French police, though not the security services, as a violent petty criminal who had amassed five convictions for violence, threatening behaviour and theft. The Paris prosecutor, François Molins, said that Lahouaiej-Bouhlel had not shown any signs of being religious until he grew a beard in the week before the attack, describing him as someone who 'ate pork, drank alcohol, took drugs and had a promiscuous sex life'.[70]

Like a number of the men in this book, however, Lahouaiej-Bouhlel's life *was* on an unchecked downward spiral in the period before he committed one of the worst terrorist attacks carried out in France by a single perpetrator. His wife, Hajer Khalfallah, who was also his first cousin, filed for divorce in 2014, listing horrendous abuse on his part; among other things, she reported that Lahouaiej-Bouhlel used to urinate on her feet, smeared faeces on the walls of their flat and slashed their daughter's soft toys with a knife. Ms Khalfallah's family was also from Tunisia but had lived in Nice for some time and the marriage allowed Lahouaiej-Bouhlel to apply for French residency, leading friends to suspect that was the real reason why he married her. Ms Khalfallah reported him to the police on many occasions, as did his mother-in-law, who was also his aunt. When the women finally managed to persuade him to move out, Ms Khalfallah was so worried about further violence that she always arranged for him to see the children in a public place, well away from her flat.

With the end of his marriage, what little stability Lahouaiej-Bouhlel had been able to maintain vanished. He lost his driving job in January 2016 when he fell asleep at the wheel, exacerbating his financial problems. He was arrested twice in the six months before the terrorist attack, the first time for hitting a driver with a wooden pallet after a traffic accident – he was given a six-month suspended sentence in March – and the second when he once again fell asleep at the wheel. His mobile phone showed he was an avid user of dating sites, using them to meet women *and* men, while some friends made lurid claims to the effect that he was a cross-dresser. Lahouaiej-Bouhlel went to a mosque for the first time a couple of months before the attack, confirming that his interest in Islam was very recent, but what really seems to have appealed to this volatile, deeply unpleasant man was material that legitimised violence.

His digital history showed that he began watching ISIS torture videos online and searched for material relating to recent terrorist attacks, avidly reading reports of the Orlando nightclub massacre; he looked for gory images of car crashes and dead bodies, showing a friend an ISIS beheading video on his mobile phone and boasting that he wasn't shocked by it. Around this time, he also began planning his own final narcissistic gesture: a suicide mission on one of the most iconic streets in the south of France. No longer able to reach the wife and mother-in-law he had been terrorising for years, he decided to kill as many men, women and children as possible, before dying himself at the hands of the police.

Summary

It has long been clear that women who leave violent partners are at risk of death or serious injury. What hasn't sufficiently been recognised until now is that abusers who can no longer hurt members of their own families might, in a small number of cases, pose a lethal threat to complete strangers. Mohamed Lahouaiej-Bouhlel, Rachid Redouane and Darren Osborne had all been thrown out by their partners in the weeks or months before they committed a terrorist attack, a humiliating blow that also deprived them of access to their primary victims; like most of the terrorists in this book, their concept of family life was founded on control and they couldn't bear the loss of it. But that is not the only common factor among this apparently disparate group of men: most of them, including Tamerlan Tsarnaev, Man Monis, Driss Oukabir and Ahmad Rahimi, were on a downward spiral when they began to plot terrorist attacks. The situations they found themselves in were entirely a consequence of their own actions, but they chose to blame their predicament on anyone but themselves. Several – notably Khalid Masood, Omar Mateen and the London Bridge attackers – espoused a particularly toxic version of masculinity, using steroids to pump themselves up and dull their reactions to the pain of their victims. Indeed, *all* of the men in this chapter displayed symptoms of insecurity, resentment and rage before they turned to terrorism, suggesting that the extremist ideology they discovered was a 'justification' for acting on pre-existing violent impulses. In most cases, the first victims of those impulses were their wives, ex-wives and children – but eventually they were transferred to the public sphere, with absolutely catastrophic consequences.

4

From Children to Perpetrators

The individuals featured in this chapter, the youngest six-teen and the oldest twenty-eight when they became involved in terrorism, have done terrible things.* Some of them are directly responsible for the deaths of total strangers, others were intercepted before they were able to carry out their plans, no doubt saving many lives. This chapter is an attempt to explain how they became so dangerous, growing up in families where extremist ideas and the use of violence were normalised. Most of them are dead or serving lengthy prison sentences, reiterating a point made many times in this book about the low value terrorists place on their *own* lives, let alone those of complete

---

* Because I am writing about individuals from the same families, I have had to use first names to differentiate siblings and parents, something that shouldn't be taken to indicate sympathy for people who are responsible for mass murder in the worst cases.

strangers. The trajectory from victim to perpetrator is starkly illustrated in most of these accounts of teenagers and young people who became terrorists, raising urgent questions about when and how we should intervene in families where it is known or suspected that domestic violence is ongoing.

Salman Abedi

On the evening of Monday, 22 May 2017, thousands of young fans filled the Manchester Arena to watch Ariana Grande perform a concert in her *Dangerous Woman* tour. The American singer is not much older than some sections of her audience and she combines stage costumes they can easily emulate – short skirts, crop tops and boots – with a modern feminist message. On the night, excited teenagers turned up with older sisters, mothers and aunts, ready to enjoy a girls' night out, while others had arranged to be picked up by their parents at the end of the performance. It was a joyous occasion, a celebration of female bonding, and the show was just finishing when a twenty-two-year-old man called Salman Abedi detonated a home-made bomb in the foyer. He had packed the bomb with nuts and bolts to cause as much damage as possible, and scenes of absolute horror followed, filling the foyer with the screams of terribly injured people as parents and children searched desperately for each other. Twenty-two people died and, inevitably, given the nature of the event, three quarters of the fatalities were female; the youngest, eight-year-old Saffie Roussos, had come to the concert with her mother and older sister, both of whom were injured.

For me, listening to news bulletins as the horrific details emerged, it was the most obviously misogynistic attack in recent history, something that also occurred to Nazir Afzal, who was chief executive of the Association of Police and Crime Commissioners at the time. He looked at the programme of events at the Manchester Arena in the period immediately before and after the concert and realised that most of them, including a heavy-metal concert and a wrestling match, would have had predominantly male audiences. 'The only one that would have had a mostly female presence was Ariana Grande's concert,' he told me. 'For me, it was a no-brainer. This man had been driven by his hatred of women and girls – and LGBT people,' he added, pointing out that the singer has a sizeable gay following.

Salman Abedi was born, went to school and lived most of his life in Manchester, making him a 'home grown' terrorist in the usual meaning of the word. Naturally people wanted to know what had made this young man turn so viciously on the city which had given his parents refuge from the Libyan dictator, Colonel Muammar Gaddafi. The death toll in the Manchester Arena bombing was the highest among the five terrorist attacks in the UK in 2017, prompting an outpouring of grief and incomprehension. It was also the attack that came nearest to being thwarted, as David Anderson's report acknowledged, albeit in somewhat opaque language:

> Although he remained a closed SOI until the day of the attack, Salman Abedi continued to be referenced from time to time in intelligence gathered for other purposes. On two separate occasions in the months prior to the attack, intelligence was received by MI5 whose significance *was not fully appreciated at the time*. It was assessed at the time to relate not to terrorism but to possible non-nefarious activity or to criminality on the part of Salman Abedi. In retrospect, the intelligence can be seen to have been *highly relevant to the planned attack*. [My italics][71]

This is in all likelihood a reference to Salman's visits, in the months before the bombing, to an ISIS recruiter and Category A (high security) prisoner, Abdalraouf Abdallah, who was serving a five-year sentence in Liverpool for terrorist offences. Salman went to see Abdalraouf on two occasions, something that emerged at the trial of his elder brother, Mohammed Abdallah, who had recently returned from Syria, on terrorist offences at the Old Bailey in December 2017. There were close links between the two families, who were both from Libya and lived in nearby streets in south Manchester: when Abdalraouf was left paralysed after being shot in the back while fighting with anti-Gaddafi forces in Libya, Salman's father, Ramadan, urged his friends on Facebook to pray for the young man's recovery.[72]

On his return to the UK, Abdalraouf ran an ISIS 'communications hub' from the family home in Manchester and helped a number of men, including his elder brother, to travel to Syria to fight for the terrorist organisation.[73] A heavily redacted but revealing report published by Parliament's Intelligence and Security Committee (ISC) eighteen months after the Manchester Arena bombing revealed that Salman's first visit to Abdalraouf needed to be approved by the prison authorities, but neither visit was considered significant. In evidence to the ISC, MI5 adopted a rueful tone: 'We wouldn't see [Salman] and [name redacted] as legitimately connected . . . They were extremist associates . . . It is reasonable to suppose . . . that the nature of that visit was a sort of junior want-to-be extremist, in the shape of [Salman], visiting someone to whom he looked up.'[74]

But even if MI5 had been unaware of Salman's visits to Abdalraouf Abdallah, the young man *was* identified by a separate 'data-washing' exercise designed to flag up individuals who merited further examination. He was one of a number of individuals whose cases were due to be reviewed at a meeting scheduled for Wednesday, 31 May – nine days *after* the bombing.

Criticism of MI5 (and the police, who knew Salman as a petty criminal) was muted after the attack, not least because most commentators on terrorism are aware of the workload both organisations have faced in recent years. Salman Abedi was one of more than 20,000 closed SOIs at the time of the bombing, and the sheer number of terrorist plots the security services had to stop in 2017 – nine between March and December alone – shows how stretched resources were at the time. But the ISC report was critical, concluding that Salman 'should have been subject to travel monitoring and/or travel restrictions' by MI5.[75]

The case for such restrictions would have been even more pressing had MI5 been aware of a specific feature of Salman's history, one which is absolutely central to the argument of this book. Five years *before* the Manchester Arena bombing, he was involved in an incident of domestic abuse which, if understood correctly, would have indicated that he was under the influence of a particularly misogynistic species of Islamist radicalisation. Yet it *didn't* result in a criminal conviction or a referral to the government's Prevent programme, which is supposed to stop individuals getting involved in or supporting terrorism – failures in procedure I will come back to in a moment.

First, some background is needed. Salman's father, Ramadan Abedi, had been a security official in Tripoli until he fell out with the Gaddafi regime, taking refuge in Saudi Arabia before setting up home in Fallowfield, an area of south Manchester popular with Libyan exiles. Salman was the family's second son, born in 1994, and a third boy, Hashem, came along shortly afterwards. Salman attended a local boys' school where he is remembered as a far from outstanding pupil, bullied by other kids and nicknamed 'Dumbo' for his protuberant ears. When the Arab Spring reached Libya in 2011, Ramadan returned to his home country, where rival rebel groups were fighting to overthrow Gaddafi. In March that year, a coalition of NATO countries, including the UK, began military intervention in Libya, imposing a no-fly zone amid claims that the regime was committing crimes against humanity. The dictator went on the run but was captured by rebels near the city of Sirte and murdered in a particularly brutal way in October 2011. Ramadan Abedi has always denied being a member of the Libyan Islamic Fighting Group, a banned Islamist organisation, but the ISC report considers it 'highly likely that Salman and Hashem's extremist views were influenced by their father Ramadan and fostered by other members of their immediate family'.[76]

Ramadan had brought his children up in a strict Muslim household but Salman underwent a transformation in his father's absence, drinking, smoking and going to parties. He also started getting into trouble, becoming part of a violent subculture in south Manchester where he reinvented himself as a 'hardman' in gangs of mainly Libyan and Somali youths. By 2012, just a year after his father went back to Libya, seventeen-year-old Salman was already known to the police as a petty criminal who had been cautioned for theft and handling stolen goods.

The conflict in Libya was rapidly becoming a vicious civil war, with a complete breakdown of law and order and thousands of extrajudicial killings. That didn't stop Ramadan inviting Salman and his younger brother Hashem to visit him on several occasions, and there is no evidence that they were kept away from the conflict; Ramadan once posted a picture on his Facebook page of the younger boy in Libya, holding a semi-automatic weapon, under the caption 'Hashem the lion . . . training'. (Six months after the bombing, the British government requested the extradition of Hashem from Libya to face charges of murdering twenty-two people, along with numerous counts of attempted murder and conspiracy to cause an explosion.) Salman posed for similar photos, excitedly handing them round to impress his friends on his return home.

Ironically, in view of what he did three years later, the British government actually rescued Salman and his younger brother from Libya in 2014, when fierce fighting erupted in Tripoli; the boys were among a group of a hundred British citizens picked up by a survey ship, HMS *Enterprise*, which had been diverted to evacuate British nationals.[77] Salman was nineteen at the time and the effect on impressionable young men of witnessing boys their own age, armed to the teeth and taking the law into their own hands, is not difficult to imagine; one former friend of the brothers said that Salman and Hashem 'saw people get killed, [and] horrific things' in Libya.[78] Another acquaintance of the family believed that the absence of his father during this period of Salman's life was significant:

[Ramadan Abedi] has basically been in Libya since 2011, since when Salman was 16 or 17. This is a time when a boy really needs his father.

Some of these young Libyan lads are pretty wild, especially those who fought in the revolution. There's a problem with some getting into gangs. Some of them are off their heads, frankly. And by leaving Salman here to continue his studies, they couldn't be sure what sort of company he was keeping.[79]

Salman had been treading a well-worn path, rebelling against a strict religious upbringing, but that didn't mean he was immune to the hard-line species of Islam he encountered in Libya, where the conflict was increasingly dominated by Salafist groups. The ISC report expressed surprise that no members of the Abedi family were ever referred to Prevent, a fair criticism in view of their regular journeys in and out of a war zone.[80] But even members of the ISC, no matter how well informed on other matters, seem to have been unaware of the specific incident in 2012 which should have brought Salman to the attention of the security services a good two years earlier than his first-known appearance on their radar.

By this point in his life, Salman was an IT student at Manchester College, a further education college for young people aged sixteen to nineteen. A couple of people who knew him at the time claimed after the bombing that they were so alarmed by his extremist views that they made separate calls to an anti-terrorist hotline. Another individual, a young man who was in the same year at Manchester College, was more specific: he recalled that Salman was a misogynist who had 'serious issues with women, especially the female staff'. The former student said: 'He wouldn't listen to them. He had a dreadful attitude and would argue with them about anything. He would hang around with other lads who would smoke weed and harass the girls. They'd say really inappropriate things, he just had no respect for women.'[81]

What happened next is recorded in David Anderson's report as 'an assault on a female while at college' but there was much more to it than that: Salman confronted a female classmate, telling her that her skirt was too short, and punched her in the head when she stood up to him. At the age of seventeen, in other words, and long before he set out to murder teenage fans in short skirts at an Ariana Grande concert, Salman was already seeking to control what women wore – and he resorted to violence as soon as his victim defied him. A young woman who witnessed the assault recalled: '[Salman] came face to face with her and punched her really hard in the side of the head. He could have killed her.'[82]

In an earlier chapter, I pointed out that misogyny is not a hate crime in this country, but assault *is* a criminal offence – and doing it in front of witnesses is evidence of an abnormally low threshold for violence. Astonishingly, however, this seventeen-year-old man who had just physically attacked a teenage girl because he didn't like what she was wearing wasn't charged with anything – and he wasn't referred to Channel, the part of the Prevent programme designed to identify individuals vulnerable to extremism, either.

Channel is not always effective in preventing terrorist attacks: Ahmed Hassan, the Iraqi teenager who tried to set off a bomb in a Tube train at Parsons Green in September 2017, had been referred to it, as had Naa'imur Rahman, who was convicted just under a year later of plotting to blow up the gates of Downing Street and behead Theresa May. But a referral to Channel *would* have given MI5 more to go on when Abedi came to their attention a couple of years later, helping to build up a picture of a violent and potentially dangerous young man.

Instead, as David Anderson's report revealed, the attack was dealt with through restorative justice, a controversial way of dealing with 'minor' offences that involves bringing the perpetrator and the victim together for a discussion about the impact of the offence. Some police forces, including the Metropolitan Police, rightly regard restorative justice as inappropriate in domestic-abuse cases and don't use it; they know that savvy offenders are all too happy to sound contrite if it means avoiding a criminal conviction and, in some cases, getting access to their children. It is hard to see how punching a woman in the head could fall into the category of minor offences but Salman was quite prepared to own up to 'anger management issues' – another popular get-out among domestic abusers. By doing so, he avoided both a criminal conviction *and* a referral to the Prevent programme, which might have begun to uncover the extent of his extremist views.

MI5 didn't become interested in Salman until July 2014, when they received a report that he had been in contact with an active SOI in the UK but decided it was a case of mistaken identity. They had another look at him in October 2015, when they had reason to believe he was in touch with a member of

ISIS in Libya, but it turned out that any contact that had taken place 'was not direct'. Even when he made another trip to Libya in 2017, a month before the bombing, nothing happened, something criticised in both the ISC report and the Anderson report. According to the latter:

> . . . despite his status as a closed SOI, an opportunity was missed by MI5 to place Salman Abedi on ports action following his travel to Libya in April 2017. This would have triggered an alert when he returned shortly before the attack, which could have enabled him to be questioned and searched at the airport by [counterterrorism] Policing under Schedule 7 to the Terrorism Act 2000.[83]

There are several qualifications in this paragraph. But the fact remains that, with no criminal convictions for violence and no referral to Channel, Salman's history looked cleaner than it was. Anderson's judgement is that it is 'unknowable' whether an earlier re-opening of the reinvestigation – before the meeting scheduled for June 2017, that is – would have allowed Salman's plans 'to be pre-empted and thwarted: MI5 assesses that it would not'. But there is no getting away from the fact that this angry, violent young man, who had brutally assaulted a woman just for wearing a short skirt, eventually carried out a terrorist attack targeted on the teenage girls who follow – and dress like – one of the world's most feminist pop stars. Salman Abedi's misogyny and record of violence against women weren't known to the people making risk assessments, a mistake that contains urgent lessons for the organisations charged with keeping us safe from terrorist attacks.

Youssef Zaghba

The third and young member of the gang that attacked London Bridge and Borough Market was a Moroccan-Italian, twenty-two-year-old Youssef Zaghba. He was born in Fez, the second largest city in Morocco, to a Moroccan father and an Italian mother who had converted to Islam after moving from northern Italy. The family had broken up by the time of the terrorist attack: Zaghba's mother, Valeria Khadija Collina, had returned to live in a village near Bologna following the break-up of her marriage while his sister, Kaouthar, who was two years older, was also living in Italy. Ms Collina was worried about her son, who had been working in London since June 2015, suspecting that he had been radicalised by material he found online. She had visited him in London and didn't like the individuals he was mixing with in east London – with good reason, as it turned out, since one of them was the MI5 suspect and soon-to-be terrorist ringleader, Khuram Butt. She last heard from Zaghba when he called her a couple of days before the atrocity at London Bridge, sounding normal and giving no indication of what he was planning.

Zaghba was never on MI5's radar, although there is very good reason to think he should have been. The Italian authorities *did* know about him and never let him out of their sight on his occasional visits to Italy, following a bizarre episode at Bologna airport on 15 March 2016, fifteen months before the attack. Zaghba wasn't the brightest would-be jihadist the security services ever had to deal with: at a time when hundreds of young men from western Europe were trying to travel to Syria to join ISIS via Turkey, he turned up at the airport without luggage and with a one-way ticket to Istanbul. When Zaghba was stopped and questioned about his intentions, he told officials frankly: 'I am going to be a terrorist.' Moments later, perhaps registering the astonishment on the faces of his interrogators, he amended his story and claimed he had meant say 'tourist'. Italian counterterrorism staff examined his phone, found Islamist propaganda videos and were convinced that he was on his way to Syria, but they decided they didn't have enough material to prosecute. Instead they began monitoring Zaghba, keeping him under surveillance all the time he was in Italy, and informed the British authorities that he might pose a risk. 'We did our best,' Bologna's chief prosecutor, Giuseppe Amato, insisted in the aftermath of the terrorist attack. 'We could just monitor him and watch him and send a note to the British authorities, that's all we could do . . . Since he moved to London, he came back to Italy once in a while for a total of ten days. And during those ten days we never let him out of our sight.'[84]

MI5's account is rather different, suggesting that the Italian authorities did tag Zaghba but with the wrong marker, identifying him as at risk of being involved in serious crime, not terrorism. The Intelligence and Security Committee report added to this picture of communication failures, highlighting an inexplicable delay in getting the Italians' request translated:

> Traces were requested on Zaghba and any contacts he had in the UK with individuals linked to Islamic extremism. The note was 'triaged'; however, it was not translated by SIS until 49 days later and, as a result, MI5 did not receive the note until six days after that. There is no record of an MI5 response, and the note was not filed in MI5's corporate system.[85]

So much confusion between allies is alarming but the end result was that Zaghba was never investigated by MI5 – even when he turned up at the Ummah Fitness Centre in Ilford and was introduced to a class at the gym by Butt, who *was* an open SOI, four months before the attack.

Whatever the shortcomings of the intelligence on Zaghba, it seems he had the classic abusive family background of a terrorist. His sister, Kaouthar Zaghba, spoke with great bitterness after the attack, describing her father's alleged violence in some detail. According to Ms Zaghba, her father was short-tempered and controlling, beating her mother and both siblings for minor infractions, as well as being determined to impose his strict interpretation of Islam on the family. She recalled: 'I fought with my father because he was violent. He hit us often. He had a violent nature, he beat me for bad marks at school, because I didn't wear the veil, for smoking a cigarette.'[86]

As soon as she was eighteen and legally able to leave Morocco, Ms Zaghba went to live with an aunt and uncle in northern Italy. After the attack, sounding shocked and extremely distressed, she told reporters she had no religion and blamed her father for the way her younger brother, whom she had been close to as a child, had turned out: 'Even when I fought with my father, [my brother] often defended me. Thinking back, maybe I think that Youssef's problems come from this. From the beatings he saw, from the endless fights, sometimes he defended my mother and took the punches that were meant for her.'[87]

As he got older, according to Ms Zaghba, Youssef changed sides and joined in his father's abuse, starting to berate his sister for wearing Western clothes. What she described is a textbook shift of allegiance, in which an abused boy separates himself from his fellow victims and starts to identify with their abuser. The future terrorist was desensitised to violence at an early age, abandoning his dangerous empathy with his mother and sister and adopting his father's patriarchal attitudes. When he met Khuram Butt and Rachid Redouane, he discovered a couple of kindred spirits, men who believed they had the right to control every aspect of women's lives. They had a great deal to bind them together: not just admiration for ISIS but the deep-seated misogyny that is integral to it – and eight people died as a consequence.

Dylann Roof

On the evening of Wednesday, 17 June 2015, a twenty-one-year-old white man turned up and asked to join a Bible-study group in the basement of a historic black church in Charleston, South Carolina. Dylann Storm Roof sat with the group in Mother Emanuel African Methodist Episcopal Church for forty-five minutes, waiting until the final prayer, when he produced a handgun and started shooting. At his murder trial, eighteen months later, the prosecution described how Roof stood over his helpless victims as they lay on the floor, shooting some of them again to make sure they were dead. Six women and two men were killed, while a third man died in hospital; the eldest victim, Susie Jackson, was eighty-seven and her twenty-six-year-old great-nephew was another of the victims. Roof fled from the church after the shootings but he was quickly identified as the chief suspect and arrested the following day in the town of Shelby, North Carolina.

After the killings, it emerged that Roof was a high-school dropout and white supremacist who had hoped to start a race war in the US. He had posted hate-filled material on a site called The Last Rhodesian, named after the former British colony, including photographs of himself posing with a handgun, holding a Confederate flag and burning the US flag. In a 'manifesto' railing against black people, he said he had deliberately chosen Charleston for the mass shooting because it was the most historic city in South Carolina and had a large black population. The then FBI director, James Comey, mysteriously declined to describe Roof's crimes as terrorism and Roof was indicted on hate-crimes charges rather than terrorist offences. The prosecution took a different view, describing Roof as 'self-radicalised' via the Internet and citing his searches for material on Trayvon Martin, the unarmed black teenager shot dead in Florida by a white neighbour who was later cleared of his murder. Bizarrely, Roof claimed that the Martin case had alerted him to the existence of what he called 'black-on-white crime', which in turn led him to discover white-supremacist sites.

Roof pleaded guilty to nine counts of murder and resisted attempts by defence lawyers to argue that he was suffering from any form of mental impairment. A psychiatric evaluation commissioned by the defence suggested he had autism spectrum disorder, anxiety, depression, paranoia and a long-standing preoccupation with racism. It said he had operated in isolation, not discussing his racist ideas with anyone but searching online for phrases such as 'Aryan Brotherhood' as far back as 2008. Roof angrily rejected the evaluation, insisting that a state psychiatrist had said there was nothing wrong with him. 'I don't have autism. I'm just a sociopath,' Roof said, according to court records.[88] His escalation from a race-obsessed loner to a mass murderer puzzled some observers, who found self-radicalisation an insufficient explanation for his horrendous crimes. 'I was not raised in a racist home or environment,'[89] he acknowledged in his rambling online 'manifesto', but it emerged after his arrest that he had grown up in a turbulent household which was eventually torn apart by domestic violence.

Roof spent much of his young life with his stepmother, Paige Mann. She married his father, a builder called Franklin Bennett Roof, usually known as Benn, in 1998 when Dylann was four and his half-sister, Amber, was eleven. The boy's family history lacked stability from the outset: his parents had been married but they divorced three years before he was born, getting back together just long enough for his mother to become pregnant but splitting again before the birth. Roof's father worked away from the family home in Columbia, South Carolina, most of the week, and his stepmother later said that she effectively raised Dylann and Amber on her own. Ms Mann described Roof as a smart but introverted boy who spent a great deal of time shut up in his room, where he looked up 'bad stuff' on his computer.[90] But it would have been hard for him to miss what was happening in the household, which Ms Mann described in court documents when she filed for divorce after ten years of marriage – an action that annoyed Roof's father so much that he employed a private detective to spy on her.

Ms Mann's affidavit claimed that the relationship was characterised by coercive control, with Benn Roof refusing to allow her to work outside the home and calling her several times a day to ask what she was doing. The couple split up in December 2008, a few months after a violent row; in court documents, Ms Mann said that her husband attacked her, pushed her to the floor and hit her on the head. She produced photographs of bruises on various parts of her body, saying she knew she had to escape the relationship. Benn Roof denied the allegations, claiming his wife was having an affair, but a divorce was granted in February 2009, with Ms Mann granted custody of the couple's daughter, Morgan. The upheavals seem to have affected Dylann's performance at school in Lexington, South Carolina, where he repeated part of a year in 2010 before dropping out altogether.

In the months before the massacre, Roof was unemployed, slept on a friend's sofa and was arrested on three occasions, including an episode when he was charged with possessing a prescription drug used to treat opiate addiction. Like several of the terrorists in the previous chapter, his life was on a downward spiral, suggesting that his childhood experience of ACEs had left him with unbearable feelings of failure and inadequacy; Roof was looking for a scapegoat and, tragically, in the Deep South, with its long history of racism, black people were an obvious target. The fact that he had admitted a drugs offence should have appeared on background checks, preventing him from buying firearms, but an error in the system meant that he was able to use money given to him by his father for his twenty-first birthday in April 2015 to buy the handgun he used to kill nine people in the church. Less than two years later, he would be sentenced to death and joined the surviving Boston bomber, Dzhokhar Tsarnaev, who is just eight months older than Roof, on federal death row.

Safaa Boular

The case of a young woman from south London, convicted of terrorism offences in the summer of 2018, is unusual for a couple of reasons. Safaa Boular achieved instant notoriety as the youngest member of the UK's first all-female terror cell, still only eighteen when she was found guilty of being the prime mover in a plot to attack the British Museum with guns and grenades. The identity of her co-conspirators made the case even more sensational: when Safaa was arrested and held in a youth detention facility in April 2017, she used a code based on *Alice In Wonderland* to encourage her elder sister and her mother to continue with plans for a terrorist attack. They both pleaded guilty to engaging in acts in preparation for terrorism, and Deputy Assistant Commissioner Dean Haydon outlined the extraordinary sequence of events that led to their arrests:

This investigation started with Safaa, and her attempts to travel out to Syria, marry a Daesh [ISIS] fighter and support their terrorist activity. Having been prevented from travelling to Syria, she then set about plotting an attack in the UK but her plans were being covered by the counterterrorism network and security services.

After Safaa was arrested and charged, her mother and sister tried to pick up where she left off. But again, working with the security services, we tracked their plans and stopped them before they were able to put them into practice.

All three women were filled with hate and toxic ideology and were determined to carry out a terrorist attack. Had they been successful, it could well have resulted in people being killed or seriously injured.[91]

This is accurate, as far as it goes, but it doesn't even begin to touch on the extraordinary family dynamics that lay behind the women's behaviour. The idea of the three of them plotting together describes the last few weeks of their relationship but not what went before, when both daughters were subjected to extreme domestic abuse by their mother – and were so desperate to escape that they separately planned to run away to Syria. If ever there was an instance of the complex victimisation I mentioned in chapter two, this is it: both girls were victims of a catalogue of crimes – physical and verbal abuse, an extreme form of coercive control *and*, in the case of the elder sister, Rizlaine, a forced marriage – long before they contemplated committing crimes themselves.

At first sight, it beggars belief that girls abused in this way became involved in a terrorist plot with the woman who caused them such anguish. But what it really shows, to anyone familiar with the psychodynamics of domestic violence, is how success-fully their mother, Mina Dich, had indoctrinated them. By the time of their arrests, these young women who once longed for a normal life could see no way out of their miserable existence other than to die for the nihilistic ideology in which Dich had immersed them; like so many abused youngsters, in other words, they ended up identifying with their abuser.

The case raises questions about the failure of child-protection procedures which should have identified the girls as being at serious risk, especially when Safaa ran away from home and called ChildLine from a local park. There was an attempt to take her into care but it failed when Dich challenged it, suggesting that interventions are not always robust enough to remove vulnerable children from households where there is persistent abuse. In chapter two, I noted that one of the effects of domestic violence on girls is to make them vulnerable to relationships with abusive men, and that is exactly what happened to Safaa. She could just as easily appear later in this book, in a section about young women who marry jihadist fighters, but she is included in this chapter because there is such an obvious link between what she suffered as a child and her eventual radicalisation. As we shall see, she was groomed at the age of sixteen by an unscrupulous British Islamist, a figure so preposterous – and yet simultane-ously so dangerous – that he would be dismissed as insulting readers' intelligence if he were a character in a novel.

Female terrorists are not unknown – Leila Khaled, the Palestinian woman who was involved in hijacking a plane in 1969, is an example – but they are rare. It also has to be said that everything that applies to pairs of brothers in this context also applies to sisters, especially when they have had the kind of isolated upbringing experienced by the Boular girls. Their mother, who was French-Moroccan, came to the UK at the age of eighteen to marry a taxi driver, Adil Boular, but the marriage broke up acrimoniously when Safaa was five and Rizlaine nine. The family lived in Vauxhall, an unassuming area of London just south of the Thames, in a street that was coincidentally opposite the headquarters of the foreign security service, MI6 (Safaa would one day be caught on CCTV outside the building, apparently assessing it as a possible target).

A photo of Dich released by the Metropolitan Police at the time of her trial shows a grim-faced woman with her hair severely pulled back from her face, in stark contrast to the glamorous younger woman with glossy brown hair who appeared in an old holiday snap with her daughters. It isn't clear why Dich, who was forty-four when she was sent to prison, turned to an extreme and eccentric form of Islam, but the police eventually found 1,500 Islamist files on her phone, including decapitation videos. By the time her daughters were teenagers, she had imposed a series of strict rules, banning them from watching TV or listening to music, isolating them from friends and insisting that they follow her example and wear conservative religious dress. She would spit at the girls and throw crockery, warning them that they would go to hell if they didn't do as they were told, and she physically attacked Rizlaine, then aged sixteen, when she posted pictures of herself in Western clothes on Facebook. 'My mother was very angry at my sister and physically abused her, hit her, and she ran away from home,' Safaa recalled during her trial. At the age of fourteen, Safaa was diagnosed with type 1 diabetes but Dich showed little interest in her younger daughter's treatment, expecting her to manage her insulin injections and trips to hospital on her own. Both girls ran away on a number of occasions but they didn't know where to get help, making them easy prey for ISIS recruiters in Syria who were looking for vulnerable individuals online.

After the catalogue of punishments she had suffered for rebelling against her mother's rules and restrictions, Rizlaine tried to find another, if very extreme, escape route. In 2014, when she was still only eighteen, she made plans to travel to Syria and got as far as Istanbul before the British police, tipped off by Safaa, asked the Turkish authorities to send her back to the UK. Rizlaine's punishment was swift and severe: not long after her return to London, Dich married her off to an imam, a much older man she met for the first time less than a week before the wedding. The marriage didn't last long, although Rizlaine did have a child with her new husband. Like many of the terrorists in this book, both girls had suicidal impulses, something that should come as no surprise in view of how many ACEs they experienced. 'In short, Rizlaine Boular embarked on this course of conduct because she wanted to die,' said her defence counsel, Imran Khan QC. 'She knew as soon as she produced a knife in the vicinity of the Palace of Westminster police officers would swoop and kill her and that's what she wanted at that time.'[92]

Safaa's own fascination with suicide was evident by the age of sixteen when the bored, lonely teenager passed the time by searching for more of the Salafist material her mother had forced her to watch online, including a photo of a woman and child wearing suicide vests. When she was stopped at the airport by the police on her return from a holiday in Morocco in August 2016, she admitted that the idea of dying as a 'martyr' appealed to her. By then, she had been using an encrypted messaging service to contact ISIS supporters and she told the police that she had between 300 and 400 ISIS friends that she'd met online. 'It was special, exciting,' she said at her trial. 'I wasn't allowed to go out with my friends. I wasn't even able to see them at school, so having friends was exciting.'[93]

Catastrophically, one of the people who got in touch was a man called Naweed Hussain, a British Pakistani in his thirties who had abandoned his wife and children in Coventry to join ISIS. Hussain was a serial sexual predator who turned up in Raqqa, the de facto capital of ISIS, in 2015 and expected to be welcomed with open arms. His new comrades took one look at their portly new recruit, however, and assigned him to caretaking duties. His pride piqued, Hussain chose the nom de guerre Abu Usamah al-Britani and posed for photos sporting a bushy beard, fatigues and mirrored sunglasses. But his main occupation was a freelance operation targeting vulnerable girls and women in the UK, whom he tried to lure to Raqqa with the promise that they would be able to marry ISIS fighters. By the time he fixed on Safaa, he had already tried to groom a twenty-nine-year-old former 'glamour' model who was suffering from depression, contacting her after she posted messages online about the impact of the Syrian civil war on children. She was shocked when her messages were intercepted by agents from MI5, who revealed to her that Hussain was in touch with a dozen other women at the same time. One of them was Safaa, who was too inexperienced to realise that she was being exploited by a serial abuser. 'He was very caring, very sweet, very flattering,' she said at her trial. 'It was the first time that I had received this kind of attention from a male.'[94]

Attention is a core element of what predators have to offer lonely young women. Hussain had plenty of time on his hands, bombarding Safaa with protestations of not-quite-undying love – what he was offering turned out to be a suicide pact – and rosy accounts of life in the caliphate. It is hard to judge how much of this relationship was fantasy on her part, bearing in mind that they had never met, but literary history confirms that the idea of a *Liebestod* – a love story consummated through death, such as the romance between Cathy and Heathcliff in *Wuthering Heights* – exerts a powerful impression on unhappy teenage girls. Despite his risible appearance, Hussain was a skilled manipulator, going out of his way to make Safaa emotionally dependent on him before revealing his true purpose – a first date in Syria on which they would wear suicide belts and blow each other up. 'Me n u in Jannah [paradise] 2gether. We depart 2 world holdin hands,' he told her, using a form of text-speak familiar to teenagers and accompanying it with a picture of himself wearing a suicide vest.[95] This plan was thwarted when Safaa was stopped at the airport and told to surrender her passport, but she had invested so much in the relationship that she agreed to Hussain's request to go through with an online wedding ceremony, conducted in the presence of two 'witnesses' in Raqqa. She even agreed to Hussain's request to send him intimate photos, a classic predator tactic that allows for the possibility of blackmail if the target tries to leave the relationship. She also agreed to keep the marriage secret, except from her immediate family. 'Rather than finding a saviour, she ended up in the hands of a monster,' Imran Khan observed at her trial.[96] Dich, however, welcomed the surprising news that her sixteen-year-old daughter had married a thirty-two-year-old jihadist who already had a wife in the UK, getting in touch with Hussain and addressing him as 'son'.

Agents from MI5, who had been monitoring Hussain's communications for some time, took a much dimmer view of the relationship. The security service employs role players who identify extremists online and join in their conversations, pretending to be jihadists themselves. With Safaa unable to travel to Syria for the moment, MI5 urgently needed to know whether Hussain had an alternative plan for her to carry out a terrorist attack in the UK, and they used a couple of undercover officers to sound out his intentions. When they told him they were interested in staging an attack in London, Hussain took the bait and sent a list of possible targets that included the O2 Arena and other landmarks. He also asked whether the role players had access to firearms or explosives, mentioning a couple of 'brothers' in the UK who were willing to take part in the plot. MI5 knew that Hussain's biological brother was in prison, convicted of sending money to ISIS, and suspected that the 'brothers' were really members of the Boular family. Their suspicions were confirmed on Safaa's seventeenth birthday, at the end of March 2017, when Hussain sent her a series of messages revealing that the target was the British Museum. MI5 had to assume that a terrorist attack on London was imminent, instigated by Hussain – and within days he was dead.

The extrajudicial killing of British jihadists in Syria by drone strikes is highly controversial. In September 2015, the then Prime Minister David Cameron announced that twenty-one-year-old Reyaad Khan from Cardiff had been killed by an RAF drone near Raqqa a month earlier, claiming that the ISIS recruiter was planning 'barbaric' attacks in the UK. Nine months earlier, Mohammed Emwazi, the Londoner better known as the masked ISIS killer 'Jihadi John', was killed while travelling in a car outside Raqqa after British intelligence supplied his whereabouts to an American air-force base in Nevada. Hussain was killed in April 2017 by a drone from the same base, also acting on information supplied by British intelligence, although the circumstances didn't emerge until almost a year later.[97]

Safaa heard about his death from one of the MI5 undercover officers, still in role, who contacted her with the 'wonderful news' that her husband had been martyred. Despite the fact that she had never met Hussain, it isn't hard to imagine the impact of this sudden bereavement on such a vulnerable young woman; she was distraught and immediately thought about staging a suicide attack, telling the role player she wanted to die and meet Hussain in paradise. When the MI5 officer asked what she and Hussain had planned, she said she didn't know the exact details of the plot but mentioned some elements of it – a Russian make of gun and a 'pineapple', the code they had used for hand grenades. She said: 'I don't know how but I want to hasten to meet my lord. He showed me a few main things with regards to the Tokarev and pineapple. He also mentioned a location. The only thing that has delayed this is getting hands on the stuff.'[98]

The MI5 agents had what they wanted, an admission of guilt, and they moved fast, arresting Safaa and charging her with engaging in acts in preparation for terrorism. The agency had had the family under surveillance for some time and intercepts of phone calls from the detention centre where she was being held revealed that Safaa was trying to persuade her mother and sister to go ahead without her, using a code based on phrases from *Alice in Wonderland*. According to evidence presented at their trial, Dich and Rizlaine duly drove around Westminster scoping out locations for a terrorist attack, bought large kitchen knives and came up with a new plan to stab a police officer. It sounded like a copycat of the Westminster Bridge attack, when PC Keith Palmer was murdered by Khalid Masood at the gates of Parliament the previous month, and the women were arrested, in separate raids, a day before the planned attack. Rizlaine confronted armed police as they forced their way into her house in Willesden, north London, and was shot in the stomach several times. She survived and both women appeared in court fully veiled for their trial, just over a year later.

Safaa was a different matter. She had abandoned her jilbab and hijab by now, dressing for court appearances in a short skirt and cardigan. No doubt it was part of the defence strategy to show that she had changed and yet she sounded sincere when she said her time in youth custody had provided her with an opportunity to meet people from different backgrounds, including boys and non-Muslims, for the first time. She and Rizlaine were both given life sentences nevertheless, and the minimum terms of thirteen and sixteen years' imprisonment mean that the prospect of any kind of normal existence is a long way off for these abused young women from a severely dysfunctional family. It is striking that their mother, who did so much damage to both her daughters, received a much shorter sentence. Mina Dich will be allowed out of prison on licence after serving less than seven years.

Syed Farook

Syed Rizwan Farook grew up in California, the son of parents who moved to the US from Pakistan. Two things stand out about Farook, a twenty-eight-year-old health inspector who carried out a terrorist attack in San Bernardino on Wednesday, 2 December 2015: his accomplice was his wife, Tashfeen Malik, twenty-nine; and the people they murdered were Farook's colleagues, who were attending a training event followed by a lunch. Farook went to the event but left early, returning half an hour later wearing a ski mask and combat gear. Malik was with him, similarly attired, and she fired first, according to survivors; when the couple left, four minutes later, fourteen people were dead and twenty-two injured. There was then a gap of four hours before police went to the couple's home, tipped off by a witness who had recognised Farook, despite his disguise. When the police arrived, Farook and Malik fled in an SUV but got less than three miles away before they were killed in a shoot-out with police.

After the attack, which was the worst in California since 1984, many questions were asked about where and how this apparently ordinary couple had been radicalised. Although it is by now a familiar pattern, many observers were shocked by the fact that Farook and Malik left behind a six-month-old daughter, who was orphaned in the shoot-out and taken into care by child services in San Bernardino.

Farook was described by family members and colleagues as a devout Muslim who went to Saudi Arabia several times, completing the hajj pilgrimage in 2013, but showed no interest in politics. Malik came from a modern family in Pakistan but had begun posting extremist messages online as long ago as 2007, when she was a pharmacology student at a university in the Punjab, as well as adopting conservative Muslim dress and attending classes at a religious academy which taught the Wahhabi form of Islam. Malik posted a message immediately before the attack, pledging allegiance to Abu Bakr al-Baghdadi and ISIS on behalf of herself and her husband, although the FBI found no evidence that they were in direct contact with any extremist organisation. Malik's history prompted speculation that she was responsible for radicalising Farook, whom she first encountered on a dating site, but the FBI discovered that they had exchanged private messages displaying a mutual enthusiasm for extremist organisations and the idea of martyrdom long before they met in person. The then director of the FBI, James Comey, confirmed the existence of the messages at a press conference after the attack.

The couple met and married in Saudi Arabia in 2014. Malik joined Farook in California a month later and they had a second wedding ceremony, possibly to satisfy immigration officials, in August that year – less than sixteen months before the massacre at Farook's workplace. The FBI concluded that they spent most of that time preparing the attack, something that suggests it was always the purpose of the marriage. Comey described them as 'home grown violent extremists', a telling phrase in view of what has emerged about Farook's lengthy childhood experience of domestic violence.

Farook's mother says she suffered years of abuse at the hands of her violent, alcoholic husband, who is also called Syed Farook. Rafia Farook repeatedly applied for restraining orders, going to court on many occasions and describing her husband as 'mentally sick' and 'abusive'. In legal documents, she listed numerous violent incidents and mentioned an occasion when her son had tried to 'save' her.[99] She claimed that Farook Senior choked her, dropped a TV on her while he was drunk, and used verbal and physical abuse against her and the children.[100] 'He is always mad,' she said in court documents. 'Drinking all day. Screaming on me, shouting at my kids for no reason.' She applied for and got a legal separation in October 2008, following an incident in February when her husband was kept in hospital for observation for seventy-two hours after he threatened to kill himself during a family row.

The younger Sayed Farook was in his late teens by the time his parents separated but even then the alleged abuse continued, with Ms Farook making another complaint about domestic violence as recently as February 2015, only ten months before her son and his wife carried out their horrific attack. There is no doubt that meeting a similarly minded extremist online was a crucial event in Farook's progress towards becoming a terrorist. But it seems this is a familiar trajectory in which a boy witnesses violence towards his mother, is unable to stop it and eventually adopts a violent persona himself, encouraged by his exposure to an extremist ideology.

Amer, Abdullah and Jaffar Deghayes

Pairs of siblings have already featured several times in this book but the tragic story of the Deghayes boys involves *three* brothers from Brighton who joined a terrorist organisation in Syria, along with a refugee from Sierra Leone who was the eldest brother's closest friend. The brothers' story follows a path through teenage gangs in this country to volunteering abroad as jihadists, a trajectory we will look at more closely in chapter five, but it appears in this section because it is such a graphic example of the effects of ACEs, including severe and persistent domestic abuse, on vulnerable boys.

The first of the Deghayes brothers to go to Syria, eighteen-year-old Amer, left the UK in October 2013, supposedly to help deliver humanitarian aid; in reality, he had gone to fight for the al-Nusra Front, one of the most feared Islamist militias in the country. Al-Nusra was accused of suicide bombings, mass executions of soldiers and massacres of civilians, and its leaders were always open about their links to AQ; in April 2013 they angrily rejected a claim by Abu Bakr al-Baghdadi that they were now part of ISIS, eventually becoming AQ's official affiliate in Syria. Al-Nusra's aim was to overthrow the widely hated dictator Bashar al-Assad and replace him not with a democratic government, as many secular opponents of the regime wanted, but with what Amer Deghayes described as the 'justice of Islam'.[101]

The Deghayes family had been known to police and social workers in Brighton for years but the authorities didn't immediately realise that Amer was in Syria or what he was doing there, which might have raised safeguarding questions about his younger brothers. Adbullah and Jaffar followed a few months later, in January 2014, along with Amer's friend, Ibrahim Kamara. The Deghayes family was from Libya and it wasn't unusual for them to be out of the country for extended periods so it wasn't until February 2014, when word reached Ibrahim Kamara's mother that her son and his friends were in Syria, that the alarm was raised. The police quickly established that all three boys had bought one-way tickets to Turkey and came to the conclusion that they had joined Amer and the al-Nusra Front. That was exactly what had happened and it was confirmed by the terrible news that arrived later the same year.

Within nine months of leaving the UK, the younger two Deghayes brothers and their friend from Sierra Leone were all dead. The first to die was Abdullah, who was shot by a sniper in Latakia, a coastal town in north-west Syria, shortly after his eighteenth birthday. Five months later, the eldest of the trio, nineteen-year-old Ibrahim Kamara, was killed in an American air strike on al-Nusra fighters in Aleppo. A month later, in October 2014, Jaffar, who was still only seventeen, was shot dead by Syrian government troops in Idlib, a town around forty miles south-west of Aleppo. Amer had been shot and wounded in the stomach during the battle that killed Abdullah, but he managed to survive his injuries. In an interview posted on Facebook a couple of years later, he said that his younger brothers 'were killed in the path of Allah' and expressed the hope that they were in paradise.

The news that three teenagers from a town on the south coast of England had died fighting for a terrorist organisation in Syria caused a great deal of heart-searching. A whole series of agencies had been involved with the Deghayes parents and children, who had been victims of a vicious and long-running campaign by racists. Later, according to a review commissioned by the Brighton & Hove Local Safeguarding Children Board, they became known as a problem family whose younger sons were involved in anti-social and criminal activities.[102] Before the catastrophic events of 2014, the brothers and their sister had been living with their mother, Einas Abulsayen, in the Preston Park area of Brighton and before that with both parents in Saltdean, a village on the eastern edge of the city. The children grew up in an area that was mostly white – comprising almost 95 per cent of the population of Brighton & Hove, according to the 2011 census – and where local residents had successfully campaigned in 2003 against the opening of a centre for asylum seekers.

Back in Libya, the Deghayes family were opponents of the Gaddafi regime, which is said to have imprisoned and murdered the brothers' paternal grandfather, a prominent lawyer, in 1980. Their own father, Abubaker Deghayes, left Libya with his wife and settled in Sussex in the early 1990s. The couple didn't find the move easy, leaving an educated, high-status section of Libyan society for an English village where they were very much outsiders. At one point they went back to Libya with the children – there were five sons and a daughter, in all – for an extended period. But they missed the UK and returned to live in the Brighton area, where Abubaker Deghayes became a trustee of one of the local mosques.

As political refugees, their lives were deeply affected by the turmoil in north Africa and the Middle East, especially after the huge publicity that surrounded the release of Abubaker Deghayes's brother, Omar, from the detention camp at Guantanamo Bay. He was held in the camp for five years after being arrested in Pakistan, and became one of many detainees who spoke out about savage treatment. Several MPs and the main Brighton paper, the *Argus*, campaigned for him to be released and the British government eventually stepped in, demanding his return, along with several other British citizens or long-term residents.

Omar was released in December 2007 and returned to the UK without ever being charged, but that didn't stop his nephews being taunted as 'terrorists' at school in Brighton. Racist graffiti was daubed on walls in their village, including the slogan 'Behead all Muslims' in twelve-inch high letters, and the family's car and house were attacked with bottles and stones.

The boys suffered physical violence as well: in September 2009, Abdullah and his twin brother Abdulrahman were beaten up on their way home from school while their eldest brother's friend, Ibrahim Kamara, was assaulted so viciously the following year that he had to spend several days in hospital. The Deghayes family reported this litany of racist threats and violence but it continued, with some evidence suggesting a targeted campaign by far-right groups. According to the Safeguarding Board review, quoting a report from a Community Safety Manager, 'in January 2013, "a group of individuals, describing themselves as members of far right groups . . . had to be removed from [redacted], having turned up with flags and megaphones shouting and falsely accusing a resident . . . of being a Jihadist and a terrorist as well as various other slanders".'[103]

It seems a little surprising that this series of events didn't lead to prosecutions, but there is only one instance of a suspect receiving a caution. What happened next is described in the dry language of the Safeguarding Board review, where Abdullah and his twin brother Abdulrahman are identified by the letters W and Q: 'Over time, siblings Q and W's behaviour changed and they began to defend themselves, retaliate and then were perceived sometimes as being the perpetrators of the incidents. From 2009 there began to be reports of the boys being involved in anti-social behaviour and crime, getting into fights.'[104]

The reality was rather more dramatic. In February 2011, Ms Abulsayen left her husband, for reasons I will return to later in this chapter, and moved to Preston Park, an area in the north of Brighton. The family's new home, in emergency accommodation provided by the council, was damp and difficult to heat. Amer, who had never been in trouble with the police, tried to stand in for his father but the twins, by now aged fifteen, were completely out of control. Abdullah and Abdulrahman formed their own gang, became well known to the local police for a series of muggings, thefts and assaults, and eventually drew Jaffar into their lifestyle. Mark Townsend, who wrote a meticulously researched article about the family for the *Guardian*, offered this succinct description of the younger boys' transformation:

> Amer watched helplessly as his other brother, Jaffar, 13, was sucked into the violence. Towards the end of 2011, staff from social services observed a dramatic turnaround in Amer's brothers, who had gone from being victims to perpetrators: 'The boys are enforcers/bullies across the city, looking for a belonging and ending up in gang culture.' Police at the time regarded the three younger brothers as a 'one family crime wave'.[105]

Obviously this development shouldn't be considered in isolation from the racist attacks the whole family had endured over a long period; this story, like that of the Boular sisters, is as much about complex victimisation as anything else. But violent behaviour by teenage boys and young men is often an indication of violence in the *home*, and it should come as no surprise that their father's alleged violence is central to the story of the Deghayes brothers.

The accusations of domestic abuse against Abubaker Deghayes were outlined in the Safeguarding Board review, which suggested that it predated the racist abuse by more than a decade. The review also described the very difficult circumstances his wife, Ms Abulsayen, had struggled with:

> Health services recognised that the mother was isolated, rarely leaving the house and wanting more help with the children. The father was often away on trips abroad. The first indication of possible domestic abuse was *in 1996* and then again in 2000, prior to the family leaving the UK for several years. On their return to the UK there were further suspicions of domestic abuse. [My italics][106]

It is clear from this official account that the alleged abuse started before the younger boys were even born. In 2010, they disclosed at a youth club that they were being physically abused by their father 'in relation to their lack of observance of their religion'.[107] An investigation produced a raft of allegations, including a claim that Abubaker Deghayes forced his sons to get up at 4.30 a.m. to study the Qur'an and punished them if he felt they weren't paying sufficient attention; this took the form of forcing them to stand against a wall for up to seven hours while he whipped them sporadically with electrical wire.[108] Scars and bruises were allegedly observed on the boys' bodies, leading social workers to conclude that Amer, the twins and Jaffar 'were subject to actual, emotional and physical harm'.

Abubaker Deghayes has always denied the allegations, claiming that they were part of a racist vendetta against him. The children were nevertheless made the subjects of child protection plans and Ms Abulsayen was advised to leave her husband. It was at this point that she moved to Preston Park, while Abubaker Deghayes was arrested on suspicion of domestic abuse and released on bail. His bail conditions forbade him from approaching his family in their new home, but the police say he persistently broke the conditions. The Crown Prosecution Service considered bringing charges but the boys suddenly withdrew their witness statements, having been 'pressurised' to do so by their father, again according to the police.[109] The CPS decided that a prosecution could not proceed without them and the child protection plans came to an end in January 2012, for reasons outlined in the Safeguarding Board review:

> [The boys] were no longer considered to be at risk of physical or emotional harm from their father as they no longer lived with him, and at that point he was no longer in the UK. This decision was taken in full knowledge of siblings Q and W's increasing involvement in anti-social and criminal activity as well as low school attendance rates. This arguably could have met the threshold for a child protection plan for neglect, as despite the mother's attempts to care for them she had little authority over them.[110]

There appears to have been a failure to understand that domestic abuse often continues, albeit in a different form, even when the parents no longer live in the same house. After their separation, there were 'no further reports of physical violence' towards Ms Abulsayen, but the Safeguarding Board review compiled after three of the couple's five sons joined the al-Nusra Front suggests that 'the coercion and control aspects of domestic abuse' continued and were compounded by her isolation and lack of support.[111] It is impossible not to feel sympathy for this single mother, on her own in a foreign country, struggling to control teenage sons who had absorbed very traditional patriarchal attitudes. This was a family where men had higher status than women and political violence was normalised; in 2006, Abubaker Deghayes was recorded telling an undercover journalist that the then Prime Minister, Tony Blair, was a 'legitimate target' for suicide bombers, along with the American President, George W. Bush.[112]

Eighteen months after his mother's move to Preston Park, Jaffar began displaying attitudes that worried the agencies which were already struggling to deal with the family. When he was arrested in the autumn of 2012, drunk and yelling abuse at passers-by in the centre of Brighton, he shouted: 'Allah will seek his revenge for me, do what you want to me, see what happens when judgement day comes, you will all go to hell.'[113] A year later, on his return from a trip to Libya – an increasingly cha-otic country, gripped by a conflict between competing Islamist factions – Jaffar made a heated remark about the Americans to a youth worker, who thought his speech and behaviour were irrational. He was referred to a Prevent panel in November 2013 but its remit was limited: the risk of young men travelling to fight overseas wasn't on the agenda in those days and, in any case, Jaffar's brother Amer was believed to be in Turkey or Libya, not Syria. The discussion focused on Jaffar, not his wider family history or the kind of people he was mixing with, and concluded there was no current evidence that he was at risk of radicalisation.[114] A couple of months later, Jaffar and his elder brother Abdullah set out to join Amer in Syria.

Sadly, the idea of a link between domestic abuse and terrorism was on no one's radar back in 2013. What we can see now – the risk to a group of angry boys immersed in a criminal subculture, with low self-esteem and a fragile sense of identity – was far less evident half a dozen years ago. As a senior police officer observed in chapter two, it is also questionable whether boys in their teens are able to visualise their own deaths. A cause such as fighting against a brutal dictator might easily have appeared to offer a way out of an intolerable situation, even if it meant joining a terrorist organisation. The result was catastrophic – and the damage done to the family over many years continues to make itself felt, even in terms of the two sons who *didn't* go to Syria.

In September 2017, Abdullah's twin brother, Abdulrahman, was jailed for two years after admitting possession of Class A and B drugs with intent to supply. Seven months later, the youngest boy, Mohammed, nineteen, was jailed for four years for drug offences. In February 2019, a murder investigation was launched after Abdulrahman was found dying from stab wounds in a crashed car in Brighton. He was twenty-two. Their father has also appeared in court several times, refusing to stand in front of magistrates on at least one occasion because of his religious beliefs. In August 2018, in a somewhat confusing outcome to a criminal trial, Abubaker Deghayes was cleared at Blackfriars Crown Court of assaulting his wife during an attempted exorcism – but was found guilty of witness intimidation. He was jailed for eighteen months for threatening to have her shot if she gave evidence in the assault case.

The couple's eldest son, Amer, was still alive in Syria at the time, having survived against the odds for almost five years. A month later, the twenty-three-year-old was reported to be one of the last British foreign fighters in Syria, holed up in Idlib with fighters from Hayat Tahrir al-Sham, the new name for a coalition of Islamist militias that includes the remnants of the al-Nusra Front. At the time, Idlib was the last stronghold of anti-Assad forces and home to hundreds of thousands of refugees from other parts of the country. Many of them loathed the jihadists as much as they did Assad, but Amer Deghayes was unrepentant. In an interview with his family's local paper, the *Argus*, he said he had no intention of leaving Idlib and feared neither death nor capture by government forces.[115]

Summary

In an earlier section of this book, we saw the impact of an accumulation of ACEs, including domestic violence and bereavement, on two boys growing up in impoverished circumstances in France. Most of the children in this chapter were likewise exposed to abuse in the home, witnessing a parent's violence – and becoming the target of it themselves, in the case of the Boular sisters and the Deghayes brothers. It shows very clearly how children are worn down by living in a violent household, no matter how much they try to resist it; the London Bridge attacker, Youssef Zaghba, followed a familiar path when he tried at first to protect his mother and sister from his father's violence, before eventually switching sides as a survival mechanism. Some of these children also experienced other ACEs, including family breakdown, and it isn't difficult to see why they sought refuge in gangs or looked for scapegoats, as Dylann Roof did with such terrible consequences in South Carolina.

The tragic story of the Boular sisters confirms that the impact of abuse is indeed different for girls, leaving the younger girl susceptible to an out-and-out charlatan who bombarded her with attention and promises of love. Hers is one of several cases in this book that raises questions about the failure of child-protection procedures in families where domestic abuse is suspected – even when a girl actually asks for help, as Safaa Boular did when she called ChildLine. In the case of the

Deghayes brothers, there seems to have been a failure to recognise that the father's extreme views placed his sons at risk of radicalisation, even though the entire family – and his alleged history of domestic violence – was known to the authorities over a long period.

A similar question arises in relation to the Manchester Arena bomber, Salman Abedi, who is the only terrorist in this chapter who *didn't* witness domestic violence in its normal sense, as far as we know. But Abedi and his younger brother Hashem were encouraged by their father to become immersed in the brutal culture of a civil war, raising the question of whether we need to expand current definitions of child abuse. Insufficient attention has been paid to the way in which Abedi absorbed what he had seen in Libya – including an Islamist culture wholly opposed to equality between the sexes – and replicated the carnage of that conflict among teenage girls enjoying a night out in his home city.

5

The World's Biggest Gang

'Gangster Islam'

When I began writing about the boys and young men who were going abroad to fight for one or other Islamist militia, I quickly realised that modern terrorist organisations like ISIS are grown-up versions of teenage gangs. Boys who join gangs are usually seeking excitement, a sense of comradeship and an identity based on strength rather than victimhood. The al-Nusra Front and ISIS offered all of that *and* the chance to act out military fantasies in a situation where the forces of law and order no longer operated. At home, gang members live with the constant threat of arrest, risking prison sentences and serving as a reminder that most outsiders and their own families regard them as little more than petty criminals. While gang membership legitimises the carrying of weapons to impress and for self-defence, the kind of hyper-masculine identity it encourages often leads to convictions for very serious crimes, including rape and murder in the worst cases. Nothing like that was going to happen in Raqqa or Mosul while ISIS was running the show and many foreign fighters exhibited a species of bravado about the prospect of dying in battle, ignoring the brutal reality of being blown apart by IEDs or drones. Some, of course, were drawn to ISIS precisely because they were depressed and self-hating, romanticising the idea of 'martyrdom' either as a shortcut to paradise or an escape from their problems.

Boys who have witnessed violence by fathers or stepfathers already have a damaged model of how to relate to other people, which they carry with them when they get involved in gangs – a substitute family, in effect. Losing a parent through separation, imprisonment or death is another risk factor, along with mental illness, one of the 'toxic trio' of ACEs mentioned in chapter two. According to a government agency, Public Health England (PHE), a study of young people who had been arrested showed that a quarter had a suspected mental illness, while one in ten male gang members was considered at risk of suicide or self-harm.[116]

Levels of self-harm and suicidal thinking are even higher among gang-affiliated girls, affecting one in three, according to PHE – an unsurprising finding in view of the fact that sexual abuse is rife in gangs. Operating within a rigid male hierarchy, girls find themselves at the bottom of the power structure, expected to perform subordinate functions such as concealing cash, drugs and weapons. They often get involved in a quest for protection, believing that a relationship with a high-status boy will make their lives safer, but nothing could be further from the truth. Even if gang-affiliated girls are not directly involved in fights and muggings, they are at risk of prosecution for offences such as possession of knives or firearms, which carry heavy prison sentences. The women's organisation Nia, which is based in east London, has studied relationships in gangs and argues that male members regard girls 'as property or objects for male use' who must unquestioningly obey boys' demands.[117] Then there is a phenomenon known as 'retaliatory' rape, whereby a gang abducts a girl associated with a rival gang and 'punishes' its members by subjecting her to serious sexual assaults. This means that gang members who went to Syria from the UK would already have been *used* to abusing women and girls, something that the leaders of ISIS encouraged on an industrial scale.

That isn't to say that boys who join gangs are any safer and the history of one member of 'the Beatles', which is described in more detail in the next section of this chapter, graphically demonstrates the damage done by and to gang-affiliated young men in London. Ninety per cent of male gang members reported being involved in violence in the last three years, according to a PHE briefing, with four out of five reporting at least three violent incidents. In a telling observation, the briefing went on to say that 'most were found to have violent attitudes and be excited by violence, yet many also feared it'.[118] It is clear from this that gang membership, while often sought as an escape from an intolerable or dysfunctional home, simply replaces one unsafe environment with another. And while it remains the case that only a minority of teenagers end up in gangs, the effects are far-reaching in communities where they are active, as we can see from a spate of fatal stabbings in London and other British cities in 2018.

This sequence of deaths has caused a great deal of speculation about police numbers, cuts to youth services and the best ways to keep teenagers out of trouble. But there is no great mystery about which boys end up in gangs and the factors that make them susceptible, such as exposure to domestic violence, also feature in the recruiting process for terrorist organisations. It has become clear in recent years that gang membership carries the additional risk of providing terrorist organisations, such as ISIS, the al-Nusra Front and AQ's east African affiliate, al-Shabaab, with a pool of angry young men who are already immersed in a criminal subculture. The proportion of would-be terrorists who've previously been involved in violent crime is striking, with fully half of ISIS fighters from European countries already known to the police.[119] This is a significant break with the past: in the 1990s, AQ recruited individuals from an educated, middle-class background who had studied practical subjects such as engineering to degree level. More recent recruits to Islamist organisations have tended to be poorly educated and drawn from impoverished inner-city communities, where they may have joined gangs for protection. Some of them know little about Islam, so much so that two British recruits to ISIS were reported to have ordered copies of *The Koran for Dummies* and *Islam for Dummies* from Amazon before they headed for Turkey.[120]

They don't all have a gang background but connections with criminal networks are useful for acquiring weapons, while experience of evading the police comes in handy when trying to avoid surveillance by the security services of several countries. The route is so well documented that it even has a name, the 'crime–terrorism nexus', and there are many examples among the Islamists who've carried out atrocities in European cities. The Toulouse terrorist Mohammed Merah, whom we met in chapter one, had more than a dozen convictions for theft, robbery and assault before he reinvented himself as a jihadist and murdered seven people. Anis Amri, the twenty-three-year-old Tunisian who used a stolen lorry to kill eleven people at a Christmas market in Berlin in December 2016, was a drug dealer with a criminal record in north Africa, Italy and Germany. On his release from a four-year prison sentence in Italy, he went on the run to avoid deportation, ending up in Germany where he was wanted by the police for a drugs-related knife attack. Amri was encouraged to stage a terrorist attack by a fellow Tunisian, a thirty-two-year-old ISIS recruiter who sent him messages urging him to murder women and children in 'acts of martyrdom'.[121] Amri's prospects were grim by the time he decided to become a terrorist and he is very likely another member of the suicidal cohort we looked at in earlier chapters, dying four days after the attack in a shoot-out with Italian police on the outskirts of Milan. ISIS released a video in which he pledged allegiance to Abu Bakr al-Baghdadi but Amri was basically a career criminal and a heavy user of recreational drugs – blood tests after his death showed traces of cannabis and cocaine – who happened to fit the profile that ISIS recruiters were looking out for.

Would-be terrorists with a history of involvement in gangs and violent crime have an abnormally high tolerance of violence, which goes some way at least to explain how they come to commit acts that are completely unthinkable to the rest of us. After the murder of Fusilier Lee Rigby in south London in 2013, one of his killers, Michael Adebolajo, twenty-eight, actually urged passers-by to film him on their mobile phones as he waved hands soaked in his victim's blood. He committed the murder with an accomplice, twenty-two-year-old Michael Adebowale, a convicted drug dealer with a long history in gangs in south-east London. Both men were Muslim converts, originally from Nigerian Christian families, who followed the crime–terrorism route via involvement in the banned Islamist organisation, al-Muhajiroun.

Adebowale had been sentenced to youth custody for drugs offences as a teenager after a shockingly violent incident in a flat being used as a crack den; he was stabbed twice and saw another teenager slashed to death in front of him, leading to a diagnosis of PTSD, hearing voices and delusions. Adebolajo was a petty crook, one of a group of youths who stole mobile phones and threatened people with knives, before he started attending ALM meetings and protests. Three years before the murder of Fusilier Rigby, Adebolajo travelled to Kenya in the hope of crossing the border into Somalia, a route favoured by Islamists who intended to fight for al-Shabaab, but he was arrested and deported back to the UK.

In the aftermath of the murder, Harry Fletcher, former Assistant General Secretary of the probation officers' union NAPO, remarked on the susceptibility of gang-affiliated young men to radicalisation by extremists. He said: 'A major concern in recent years has been the crossover between criminal groups and Islamist organisations . . . The Islamist groups will exploit both the gang members' psychological and economic vulnerability. They'll offer them money or drugs if they're poor or the chance of salvation if they're mentally fragile.'[122]

The connection has been particularly stark in Molenbeek, a suburb of Brussels which was home to the Islamist cells that carried out the terrorist attacks in Paris in November 2015, and those at the airport and a metro station in Brussels four months later. The Moroccan-Belgian journalist Hind Fraihi, who recognised the 'crime–terrorism nexus' more than a decade ago, posed as a sociology student for three months to study Islamist infiltration of Molenbeek, coining the phrase 'gangster Islam' to describe what she found. She argued that the jihadists recruited among gang members and young men with criminal records because they wanted to exploit their access to guns and safe houses. 'Mix this with a little Islam, and this is what you get in Molenbeek,' she wrote.[123]

Salah Abdeslam, one of the suicide bombers who attacked the Stade de France in Paris, was a well-known criminal from Molenbeek with a record of theft, drug dealing and armed robbery. Abdeslam survived the attack – it's not clear whether his suicide vest failed to explode or he changed his mind and dumped it – and is now serving a long prison sentence in France. He ran a bar with his brother, Brahim, until it was closed for alleged drug dealing about six weeks before the November 2015 attacks; on the night of the Stade de France and Bataclan Theatre attacks, Brahim Abdeslam blew himself up outside the Comptoir Voltaire café in Paris.

The composition of the gang illustrates the enormous influence of a single Islamist, a small-time crook called Khalid Zerkani who came to Brussels from Morocco and became a prolific recruiter of terrorists. Zerkani, who was in his early forties, encouraged dozens of young men to commit thefts and robberies, recruiting more than seventy jihadists in the process. One of them was Abdelhamid Abaaoud, a close friend of Salah Abdeslam and another member of the gang from Molenbeek, who died in a gun battle with police in the Saint-Denis area of Paris. Zerkani had 'perverted an entire generation of youngsters, particularly in the Molenbeek neighbourhood,'[124] according to the Belgian federal prosecutor, Bernard Michel. A report from the International Centre for the Study of Radicalisation (ICSR), based at King's College, London, makes a similar point: 'More than any other example, the structures that [Zerkani] created illustrate the near-perfect merging of criminal and terrorist milieus that took place in Belgium and help explain why this relatively small country has produced nearly 500 jihadist foreign fighters in just four years.'[125] Zerkani is currently serving a fifteen-year prison sentence in Belgium, increased on appeal from twelve years to reflect the extent of his activities in recruiting terrorists.[126]

The boundaries between gang members, petty criminals and terrorists are porous; for some young men with nothing to look forward to but a revolving door in and out of prison, it is not hard to see that reinventing themselves as jihadists might offer some kind of larger meaning. The ICSR report identified a small number of recruits to terrorist organisations who were explicitly searching for a 'redemption' narrative, hoping to compensate for a criminal history by dying for a cause; it mentioned Rayat al-Tawheed, an organisation formed by British jihadists in Syria which deliberately targeted troubled young men with the slogan 'sometimes people with the worst pasts create the best futures'.[127] But many more foreign fighters were attracted by ISIS propaganda precisely *because* it told individuals who had acquired criminal records, and quite possibly been disowned by family members, that there was nothing wrong with using violence – the perfect message for men whose sense of self depended on maintaining an aggressive masculine image. We've already seen how a number of foreign fighters posted pictures of themselves with props such as combat gear,

AK-47s and rocket launchers, but some went much further and included dismembered body parts. It is clear that ISIS removed the last vestiges of restraint that might otherwise have held its recruits back from torture, rape and murder.

Everything we know about ISIS suggests that it was as much a criminal gang as a terrorist organisation, looting expensive military equipment, murdering members of rival militias and stealing large sums of money. It was always going to attract psychopaths, a label that certainly seems to fit some of its recruits from the UK – Abdel-Majed Abdel Bary, for example. Bary was (we don't know if he's still alive) a British-Egyptian rapper from west London whose father, Adel Abdel Bari, had been a senior figure in AQ. (Bari was one of the men convicted in relation to the US embassy bombings in east Africa in 1998 which killed more than 220 people, and he is currently serving twenty-five years in an American prison.) Before he fled to Syria in 2013, Bary's lyrics hinted at involvement in violent crime in west London ('blood on my hands') and on his arrival in Raqqa he embraced ISIS's culture of sadistic violence with relish. In August 2014, he posted a gruesome picture of himself holding up a severed head with the caption 'Chillin' with my homie or what's left of him'.

Partly as a result of his repellently casual attitude to decapitation, Bary briefly emerged as a possible candidate when Western security services were frantically trying to identify 'Jihadi John', the fighter who began appearing in a series of horrific ISIS videos in the summer of 2014. In fact, it didn't take long to establish that the man threatening hostages with a knife was twenty-six-year-old Mohammed Emwazi, another ISIS recruit from west London, although that didn't become public knowledge until the following year. Emwazi was a key member of 'the Beatles', so named by their prisoners because of their English accents, and all four came from a small area of west and north-west London where a violent gang culture had flourished since the 1990s, creating what the *New York Times* called 'a conveyor belt into jihadism'.[128] Three of them had links with gangs and they were also associated with the London Boys, a highly influential network of jihadists who raised funds and sent young men to train with AQ and al-Shabaab in east Africa. While one of 'the Beatles' would later claim to a British journalist that he had become 'desensitised' in Aleppo, it seems more likely that their prior involvement in gangs in the UK prepared the ground for the wave of beheadings and other atrocities that they carried out in Syria.

'The Beatles'

In December 2011, an Iranian man identified only by the initials C.E. went to the High Court to challenge a control order imposed on him by the then Home Secretary, Theresa May. The government's lawyers maintained that C.E. had attended a terrorist training camp in Somalia led by Harun Fazul, one of

AQ's most important figures in east Africa and the suspected mastermind of the 1998 embassy bombings (Fazul had been killed in a shoot-out at a checkpoint in Mogadishu six months before the hearing). C.E. complained about the impact of the control order on his family but he had a wearily familiar Islamist profile: he was separated from his wife and the government's lawyers pointed out that he had 'not always had an unwavering attachment' to his family, having left the country the day after his first child was born in 2006 to undergo terrorist training in Somalia.[129] His aim, according to the government's lawyers, was not to carry out terrorist attacks in the UK but to recruit young men on behalf of AQ and al-Shabaab. They provided a list of C.E.'s associates in London, claiming that:

The Secretary of State maintains that she has reasonable grounds for suspicion that since his return to the United Kingdom in February 2007 CE has continued to associate regularly with *members of a network of United Kingdom and East African based Islamist extremists* which is involved in the provision of funds and equipment to Somalia for terrorism-related purposes and the facilitation of individuals' travel from the United Kingdom to Somalia to undertake terrorism-related activity. [My italics]

The document went on to list ten men by name and a couple more under code names, providing a *Who's Who* of suspected Islamists from west and north-west London – the London

Boys network, in other words. One of the names was that of Mohammed Emwazi, who would eventually be identified as 'Jihadi John'. He had flown to Tanzania with two other men in 2009, ostensibly to go on safari after he finished his course at Westminster University, but all three were suspected of intending to travel to Somalia via Kenya to join al-Shabaab. They were refused entry on arrival at Dar es Salaam airport at the request of British intelligence, according to the Tanzanian police, which suggests that Emwazi had already come to the attention of MI5.

Deported back to the UK and questioned, Emwazi denied that he had been trying to reach Somalia and later complained bitterly about being under surveillance, claiming that the security service had tried to recruit him. Whatever the truth of that, what isn't in dispute is that in 2013 he disappeared to Turkey, this time with the well-worn cover story that he was going to work with Syrian refugees. Four months later, police arrived at the family home in north-west London and revealed that Emwazi had joined ISIS, which had by now displaced AQ and al-Shabaab as the most popular terrorist organisation for Western recruits. For the next few months, Emwazi's involvement with ISIS was known only to a small group of people, including the Western hostages who had the misfortune to be tortured by him and the other 'Beatles' in the basement of a house in Aleppo. A French journalist, Didier François, who was released by ISIS in April 2014, described Emwazi as 'one of the worst, who hit and tortured without the slightest restraint'.

He said: 'Between us, we called them the Beatles because we didn't know their names. There was Paul, Ringo and George; Emwazi had the name John. He was the tallest, the calmest, but also the most determined, without the slightest scruple.'[130]

A Spanish journalist, Javier Espinosa, recognised his captors as prime examples of the crime–terrorism nexus, scornfully describing them as a group of thugs who knew nothing about religion. Mr Espinosa was subjected to a mock execution by Emwazi, who pressed a gun to his head and 'fired' it three times before threatening to shoot another Spanish hostage.

'Jihadi John' first came to the attention of the wider world on Tuesday, 19 August 2014, when a four-minute video was released showing an American photojournalist, James Foley, kneeling in an orange jumpsuit before being beheaded off screen. It was a horrifying example of psychological torture, causing huge distress to Mr Foley's family and friends and marking a new low in ISIS's dehumanising treatment of helpless captives. It was followed by more videos which showed the final minutes of another six hostages: the British aid workers Alan Henning and David Haines; another American journalist, Steven Sotloff; the American aid worker, Abdul-Rahman (formerly Peter) Kassig; and the Japanese journalists, Haruna Yukawa and Kenji Goto. All of them were murdered although only a single video, showing the massacre of more than twenty captured Syrian soldiers, featured actual decapitations on screen – one of them carried out by 'John'. The revelation months later that the cold-blooded killer in the videos was an apparently ordinary computer-science graduate from north-west London caused astonishment, but his history turned out to have features common among recruits to ISIS.

Emwazi went to a secondary school in St John's Wood, the affluent area of London where another prominent member of the London Boys network, Bilal al-Berjawi, grew up after his family arrived from Lebanon. (Berjawi later became a leading figure in AQ in east Africa, dying in a drone strike on the out-skirts of Mogadishu in January 2012, just hours after his wife gave birth to a child in a London hospital – another example of a terrorist with a somewhat detached approach to paternal responsibility.) But the Emwazi family home was on the Mozart Estate, a dense area of social housing in Queen's Park, an area of London fought over by rival gangs from Kilburn and Ladbroke Grove. Some teachers remembered Emwazi as a shy boy but former students from the school told a different story, claiming that he was involved in gangs by the age of thirteen.[131] They said he was uncomfortable around girls, covering his mouth with his hand when he spoke and becoming 'obsessed' with a Muslim girl in his class; he was accused of 'borderline stalking' her and sent to anger management classes because of his dis-ruptive behaviour. He was certainly known to the police, who suspected Emwazi and his younger brother, Omar, of stealing expensive bikes to order, although they didn't manage to get a conviction on the two occasions the elder Emwazi was taken to court (Omar Emwazi wasn't so lucky, pleading guilty to handling stolen goods in August 2012). But in 2008, while he was still a student, and in a development that speaks volumes about the kind of individuals he was mixing with, Mohammed Emwazi *was* involved in a revenge kidnapping against a couple of boys who had beaten up his younger brother. Accompanied by 'two religious guys with beards',[132] Emwazi abducted the boys at gunpoint, forced them to take off their clothes and dumped them on the M1. It is pretty clear that he had been radicalised by then, attending the same mosque in Ladbroke Grove as two other men who would eventually be identified as members of 'the Beatles', Aine Davis and Alexanda Kotey.

It's not clear whether they knew each other at this time but the Counter Extremism Project, which tracks connections between Islamists, has identified all three as members of the London Boys. Kotey is the son of a Ghanaian father, who reportedly killed himself when the boy was three years old, and a Greek-Cypriot mother who brought him up in the Greek Orthodox Church before he converted to Islam. He is the only member of 'the Beatles' who didn't have gang connections during his time in London and he left the UK much earlier than the others – in 2009, on an aid convoy to Gaza, when he travelled with two more members of the London Boys. But the US State Department, which designated him a terrorist in 2017, has accused Kotey of engaging in 'exceptionally cruel torture methods, including electronic shock and waterboarding'.[133] It also named him as an active recruiter for ISIS who was responsible for persuading several UK nationals to join the terrorist organisation.

The two remaining members of 'the Beatles', Davis and El Shafee Elsheikh, had a long history of involvement in gang culture before they went to Syria. 'Paul', as Davis became known by his victims in Aleppo, was born in Hammersmith where his father, who was from Gambia, had thirteen children with four different women. Davis spent part of his childhood with his grandmother in west Africa but settled in London at the age of seventeen, embarking on a life of selling drugs, joining a gang and acquiring a string of convictions for possession of drugs and firearms. He was a classic domestic abuser, fathering four children by two women, and abandoned his Moroccan wife Amal el-Wahabi when he went to Syria.

Davis had targeted el-Wahabi when he spotted her in tears at the mosque, sensing her vulnerability, only to dump her two months before the birth of their first child in 2009; he revived the relationship two years later and they had a second child, but Davis abandoned el-Wahabi again when he fled to join ISIS. As if she hadn't suffered enough, he then tried to pressurise her into bringing their children to Turkey, threatening to take another wife unless she made the trip. He also told el-Wahabi to start collecting money for ISIS, with disastrous results: when el-Wahabi attempted to trick a friend into smuggling the cash into Turkey on her behalf, she was arrested and tried for supporting a terrorist organisation. The judge, Nicholas Hilliard QC, told el-Wahabi that Davis had 'no true regard' for her and described her children, by now aged five and seventeen months, as 'innocent victims' of their parents.[134] In August 2014, el-Wahabi was convicted and sent to prison for twenty-eight months, becoming the first person in the UK to be convicted of funding terrorism in Syria. By then her husband was on the way to becoming one of the world's most wanted men and would in time be accused, along with the other 'Beatles', of beheading almost thirty men.

It isn't clear which of the two remaining members of 'the Beatles' was George and which Ringo. But El Shafee Elsheikh was just as sadistic as the others – perhaps even more so, judging by the US State Department's jaw-dropping account of his behaviour towards hostages:

El Shafee Elsheikh travelled to Syria in 2012, joined al-Qa-eda's branch in Syria, and later joined ISIS. In May 2016, Elsheikh was identified as a member of the ISIS execution cell known as 'The Beatles', a group accused of beheading more than 27 hostages and torturing many more. Elsheikh was said to have earned a reputation for waterboarding, mock executions, *and crucifixions* while serving as an ISIS jailer. [My italics][135]

It should come as no surprise to learn that, long before he left London, El Shafee was involved in a series of extremely violent incidents that led to his elder brother being tried for murder.[136] Indeed the story of the Elsheikh boys is a classic example of the brutalising effect of gang culture, showing the interchangeability of perpetrators and victims, and preparing the two younger brothers to become foreign fighters in Syria.

The boys' parents were communists who fled a repressive Islamist regime in Sudan, coming to west London as refugees and settling in White City, just up the road from Aine Davis in Hammersmith. Their father left a couple of years later, leaving his wife to bring up their three sons – El Shafee was the middle child – on her own. He was by all accounts a quiet boy, a Queen's Park Rangers fan who studied engineering at Acton College before getting a job as a car mechanic in a local garage; he also used to do casual work with the travelling fairs that set up on Shepherd's Bush Green on bank-holiday week-ends. But his elder brother, Khalid, was moving in dangerous circles, having become friends with a much younger boy called Nathan Harris, who was a virtual crime wave in his own right. Seven years younger than Khalid, Harris was a member of a notorious gang called IOC or 'Instruments of Cruelty', and was well known to the police who suspected him of being involved in very serious crimes, including rape and murder.

In 2008, when El Shafee was nineteen, he was stabbed and seriously injured in a fight, prompting Khalid Elsheikh to set out in search of revenge. He launched an attack on his younger brother's suspected assailant, a drug dealer called Craig Brown, and part of the elder Elsheikh's ear was bitten off during a violent struggle. This led to a much more serious and indeed fatal attack on Brown, who was shot dead while visiting his girlfriend on Christmas Eve. Several boys and young men, including Khalid Elsheikh and Harris, who was still only fifteen years old, were charged with Brown's murder. They were tried at the Old Bailey in the autumn of 2009, at the end of which Harris was convicted and given a life sentence. Khalid, by then aged twenty-two, was acquitted of murder but found guilty of possessing a firearm with intent to endanger life. He was sent to prison for ten years, an event which had a traumatic effect on his younger brothers.

Within a couple of years, El Shafee was listening to recordings of sermons by radical preachers, had grown a beard and was distributing Islamist leaflets outside Shepherd's Bush market. His mother, who had left Sudan to get away from radical Islam, was dismayed by his transformation and even more worried when El Shafee persuaded his brother, Mahmoud, to attend the mosque with him. Her worst fears were confirmed in April 2012 when El Shafee disappeared to Syria and Mahmoud, who was only seventeen at the time, soon followed. In 2015, Mahmoud Elsheikh was killed fighting for ISIS near Tikrit in Iraq. El Shafee Elsheikh, who had two wives with him in Aleppo while he tortured Western hostages, named his son after his dead brother.

Three of 'the Beatles' are now in captivity and the fourth, Emwazi, died in the American drone strike referred to in chapter four. Aine Davis, who fled as ISIS began to lose swathes of territory in Syria, got as far as Turkey where he was captured and put on trial for planning a terrorist attack in Istanbul; he was convicted and sentenced to seven and a half years in prison, where he remains at the time of writing. The British government confirmed that El Shafee Elsheikh and Alexanda

Kotey were stripped of British citizenship after being captured in northern Syria by the Syrian Democratic Forces, an alliance of Kurdish and Arab forces opposed to ISIS, leading to an international row about where they should be put on trial. Complaining about losing their British passports, and shorn of the status they enjoyed as swaggering jailers in Aleppo, they cut sorry figures in interviews conducted from prison. But the bravado of ISIS's foreign volunteers was always founded in insecurity and a toxic form of masculinity, leaving them in limbo once the caliphate collapsed and the leaders of the world's biggest gang went on the run.

6

Misogyny Inc.

Teenage dreams

The image of three teenage girls striding towards the departure gates, captured on a CCTV camera at Gatwick airport in February 2015, has been reproduced many times in discussions of the role of women in the caliphate. On the day they passed the camera there was nothing to ring alarm bells, just three friends who appeared to be heading off for a half-term holiday or a study break to do some revision for their GCSEs. No one suspected that Amira Abase and Shamima Begum, both fifteen, and Khadiza Sultana, who was a year older, were about to give up everything – family, school, careers – to board a flight to Istanbul and make the hazardous journey across a war zone in Syria to join ISIS.

All three were outstanding students at their school, Bethnal Green Academy in the east end of London, so the realisation that they were on their way to start new lives in Raqqa caused not just shock but outrage. Anxiety about their future in a city strewn with corpses and rubble from air strikes was in surprisingly short supply, as though teenage girls consume news in exactly the same way as middle-aged adults who read the *Independent* or the *Sunday Times* and should have known exactly what awaited them in Syria. Nor did it seem to have occurred to the girls' critics, some of whom used quite cruel language, that the offer ISIS recruiters made to potential female volunteers was very different from what they offered young men, focusing on the 'advantages' of traditional marriage. One particularly horrible example appeared in the *Spectator* where Rod Liddle affected to be worried about the plight of Amira Abase, 'who fled the country on 17 February in order to take up an exciting and challenging position as an in-house whore for the vibrant and decapitating warriors of Islamic State'.[137] Even the usually liberal *Independent* published a piece by its columnist Grace Dent who roundly told the girls, 'you shouldn't be allowed back into the country ever, when surely there are dozens of other bloodier, more depressing places that suit your lifestyle choice better'.[138] Changing their minds wouldn't be allowed, even when they discovered the hideous reality, as they were bound to do, of living according to the rules of a singularly misogynistic terrorist organisation.

Such sneers are easy to write and fill columns with but

they fail to take into account the way teenagers acquire and use information. For a generation growing up in the first decades of the twenty-first century, the Internet and social-media sites have displaced traditional news outlets such as national newspapers and the BBC. Constant attacks on the mainstream media, derided as the 'MSM', created an atmosphere of suspicion and distrust which was skilfully exploited by terrorist organisations. ISIS recruiters, in person and via the Internet, went out of their way to sow distrust of news reports that showed the organisation in a bad light, denouncing them as attempts by Western media to demonise the caliphate. In an atmosphere in which millions of people apparently believe that the moon landings were faked, even the most horrific material can be explained away as a smear. People who assumed that the Bethnal Green girls knew exactly what they were letting themselves in for didn't stop to consider the likelihood that they had been radicalised – brainwashed, to use the language of previous generations – and deceived as ruthlessly as the underage girls targeted by 'grooming' gangs in British towns and cities. Sara Khan, founder of the anti-extremism organisation Inspire and later head of the government's commission for countering extremism, said as much in an article for the *Independent*:

Just like child abusers groom their victims online and persuade them to leave their homes and meet them, male jihadists contact women through social media and online chatrooms, and build trust with them over time. And, like child abusers, they deploy flattery and false notions of love and desire. Their targets often believe their jihadist fighter 'loves' them and considers their relationship to be genuine. They don't see themselves as victims.[139]

Nazir Afzal, the former Chief Crown Prosecutor for the North-west who led the team that successfully prosecuted members of a 'grooming' gang in Rochdale, made a similar point: 'Grooming for sex, ideology, violent crime – it's all the same,' he told me. Indeed there are parallels between the methods used by ISIS to lure girls and young women to the caliphate, deliberately sugar-coating what they would find on arrival, and those used by sex traffickers in western Europe. Victims of sex traffickers believed they were travelling to fill vacancies in bars and restaurants in London, Paris or Madrid, only to discover that they were going to be forced to have sex with dozens of strangers in pop-up brothels.

The purpose of the deception of teenage girls and young women by ISIS was different, but its recruiters offered an idealised picture of marriage and motherhood in the caliphate which was equally far removed from reality. There is nothing surprising about this: misogyny is adept at disguise and an imbalance of power between the sexes is often dressed up under the guise of 'traditional values'. It is not unusual to hear women who have left abusive relationships say that they didn't realise for years that they *were* being abused, especially when it takes the form of coercive control, and many teenage girls lack the maturity and experience necessary to see through vague claims about 'respect' and 'protection'. In addition, many of the teenage girls targeted by ISIS were from immigrant families, caught between the conservative values of their parents and a secular modern culture with relaxed attitudes to clothes, extramarital sex and gay marriage. A survey commissioned by the BBC's Asian Network in 2018 suggested that British Asians were more socially conservative than the wider UK population, especially in the area of sex and relationships: more than a third (34 per cent) would be offended if a relative had sex outside marriage, compared to 5 per cent of the general population, and slightly more (36 per cent) thought that same-sex relationships were unacceptable. They were also more religious, with almost half of British Asians saying religion was 'very important', compared to only 12 per cent of the wider population. The conflicts between the values children from ethnic minorities learn at home and those they encounter at school, on TV and the Internet add complex layers to the usual anxieties experienced by teenagers.

From the moment they left the country, it should have been obvious that the three Bethnal Green girls had been groomed by ISIS recruiters. Two were from British-Asian families and the family of the third, Amira Abase, was from Ethiopia; what's more, Abase had already been exposed at an impressionable age to extremist ideas by her own family. Her father, Abase Hussen, was filmed in 2012 in the midst of a mob burning a flag outside the American embassy, an event also attended by the hate preacher Anjem Choudary and Michael Adebowale, who went on to kill Fusilier Lee Rigby the following year. Hussen admitted he had taken his daughter to a couple of protests, including one outside the Saudi embassy which was said to have been organised by the banned Islamist organisation al-Muhajiroun, when she was only thirteen. It seems likely, however, that peer pressure played an equally significant role in the girls' radicalisation; when they went to Syria, they were following in the footsteps of one of their closest friends, fifteen-year-old Sharmeena Begum (who shared the same surname but was no relation to Shamima Begum).

Sharmeena was a vulnerable teenager who had suffered a series of tumultuous events in the year before she fled to Syria, from her mother's death from lung cancer at the age of only thirty-three to her father's remarriage a few months later. She was just the kind of troubled girl ISIS was looking for and when she bought a plane ticket for Turkey in December 2014, she showed her school friends – who might otherwise have regarded going to Syria as an unattainable dream – that it could be done. After her departure the police interviewed seven of her friends, including the three girls who followed in February, and asked them to give letters to their parents, warning them about Sharmeena's flight to Syria, but they were never delivered. The police *did* act after the disappearances in 2015, however, going to court and obtaining travel bans on five more girls from the same school – an illustration of how widely the fantasy about life in the caliphate had spread. It was a reminder that close-knit groups create their own reality, in this case preferring to stick with their view of the caliphate as a pre-feminist paradise rather than being influenced by news reports about its extreme brutality.

One of the unusual aspects of ISIS, compared to other contemporary terrorist organisations, was its explicit rejection of Western feminism. Exploiting the anxieties of girls and young women caught between two cultures, it denounced the idea of equality between men and women and praised traditional sex roles. A manifesto published online in Arabic in 2014 by ISIS's de facto women's police force, the al-Khanssaa Brigade, argued that feminism had forced women out of their natural state and blurred the difference between the sexes. It insisted that men and women needed to return to the roles they enjoyed in an idealised past, when the fundamental purpose of women was motherhood. Cynically exploiting the existence of high levels of domestic violence in the West, including the abuse some girls would have witnessed in their own families, it argued that husbands in the caliphate would treat their wives with dignity and respect:

The average Muslim man should not exploit his position to overpower or hurt. The average Muslim man is characterised by goodness and sympathy towards the weak. This was the normal way for the average man, even infidels, which would mean they should rise above harming women and criticise those who do, detract against and vilify them.[140]

At a stroke, going to live in the caliphate would erase anxieties about sex roles, parental expectations, family conflicts – and women were offered the bare-faced lie that they would actually be safer in cities run by ISIS than they were in the West. The authors of the document claimed to have visited a number of areas controlled by ISIS, including Raqqa, where they admired its 'enchanting' buildings and gardens, and insisted (in language that translators clearly had to struggle with) they had found a veritable paradise for women:

> Al-Khanssaa Media travelled these lands to check on the happy situation that Muslim women face and their return to what was there at the dawn of Islam and the black robes that enrage the hypocrites and their friends, and the good news that this situation gives regarding development and ascendance to the summit of this glory throughout the expansion of the State of Muslims and the longer it remains, we see it growing and strengthening by the hour . . .[141]

In chapter four, we saw how the jihadist from Coventry, Naweed Hussain, used the vocabulary of romance to try to entrap Safaa Boular and a whole series of other British women whom he regarded as potential brides for foreign fighters. But ISIS also employed female recruiters such as Aqsa Mahmood, originally from Scotland, who became notorious for her attempts to recruit girls and young women online from her base in Raqqa. Female recruiters used chatty advice to make life in Syria sound as normal as possible, advising girls to bring the vitamins they would need to take when pregnant and invoking a pioneer spirit to make it sound more like an adventure than joining a terrorist organisation. Mahmood even posted a list of what to pack for the trip to Syria on her Tumblr site, suggesting they might like to bring underwear that would please waiting bridegrooms. Linda Wenzel, who was only fifteen when she ran away from a town in eastern Germany to join ISIS in Iraq, recalled after being captured by Iraqi forces that she was shown videos 'where men and their wives and children wandered together through parks . . . they baked bread together. It was like being in another world'.[142]

The propaganda was extremely effective: a report published by the Institute for Strategic Dialogue in 2015 described the number of Western women travelling to join ISIS as 'unprecedented', suggesting that they already accounted for more than 550 of the organisation's 4,000 foreign recruits.[143] But the pace of foreign recruitment was about to step up exponentially: three years later, a report from the International Centre for the Study of Radicalisation suggested that up to 4,761 of the nearly 42,000 foreigners who joined ISIS between April 2013 and June 2018 were women, while another 4,640 were minors.[144]

The fact that more than a fifth of foreign recruits to ISIS consisted of women and children is breathtaking, although it has to be said that not all of the women went voluntarily; journalists who interviewed the foreign wives of ISIS fighters in detention camps in Iraq after the collapse of the caliphate found a number of women who said they had been forced to make the journey by their husbands. Some might be lying in the hope of being allowed to return home but there is no doubt that would-be jihadists from countries where patriarchal attitudes are intact, such as Morocco, Tunisia and Egypt, would have expected their wives and children to do as they were told. The fact remains that in the period between 2015 and 2016, when the flow of foreign recruits to ISIS was at its highest, women accounted for around one in three foreigners travelling to the caliphate from western Europe, including the UK and France. More than 700 children are known to have been born to women who had relationships with ISIS fighters, most of whom are trapped with their mothers in miserable detention camps in Iraq and Syria.

Young women who were deceived by evocations of an ideal Muslim state were in for a shock when they arrived in towns and cities captured by ISIS. Linda Wenzel's account of how she became disillusioned is no doubt self-serving, provided at a time when she was trying to avoid having to serve a long prison sentence in Baghdad. But her description of what awaited her when she reached Turkey chimes with the accounts of other women from western Europe whose fantasies were met with a chilling dose of reality. Wenzel, who didn't speak Arabic, was required to marry a Chechen fighter she had never encountered in person, in a ceremony conducted by phone. She wasn't told her husband's full name and they didn't have a language in common; even when they finally met, he left her on her own to cook and clean in a series of apartments in Raqqa and Mosul. Wenzel was soon widowed, following her husband's death in an air strike, and she complained about feeling lonely and isolated, although she does at least seem to have avoided being married off to another fighter. Some so-called 'jihadist brides' were less fortunate, with reports of women being married and widowed as many as half a dozen times, an experience which bears some resemblance to the multiple sexual partners imposed on victims of sex trafficking. Contrary to ISIS propaganda, domestic abuse was rife and wives had to accede to their husbands' wishes in everything, including the punishing regimes imposed on children.

In her book *Two Sisters: Into the Syrian Jihad*, the Norwegian journalist Åsne Seierstad describes what happened to a Norwegian-Pakistani woman from Oslo when she agreed to become the second wife of Bastian, a foreign fighter based in Raqqa. Predators have a sixth sense when it comes to finding fresh victims, and Aisha had already been in an abusive marriage before she married her new husband in a ceremony conducted via Skype while she was still in Norway. When she arrived in Syria with her young son, Aisha found herself in a familiar situation as Bastian began to assault her and the child, who was called Salahuddin. Seierstad writes:

Bastian locked her indoors. He locked her out of the house. He hit her. Worst of all, he beat Salahuddin . . .

When Aisha tried to protect her son, when she screamed at her new husband, he just pushed her aside . . . Salahuddin was going to be a Cub of the Caliphate, and thus he needed to be disciplined from an early age. The boy was not yet two years old.[145]

The fate of the three Bethnal Green girls who followed their friend to Syria was predictable. Within weeks of their arrival in Raqqa, all three were married off to ISIS fighters even though two of them were below the legal age for marriage in the UK. In such grim circumstances, it didn't take long for the eldest, Khadiza Sultana, to realise she had made a terrible mistake. She managed to call her elder sister in London, via a secret mobile phone, and told her that she wanted to come home. Khadiza's sister assured her that the then Metropolitan Police Commissioner, Sir Bernard Hogan-Howe, had stated publicly that none of the girls would be prosecuted if they managed to return to London.

But getting away from ISIS was no easy matter – Khadiza compared it to trying to escape from Alcatraz – and the fate of another teenager who tried to escape, seventeen-year-old Samra Kesinovic, stopped her in her tracks. The Austrian girl, who was the daughter of Bosnian refugees in Vienna, ran away with a friend to join ISIS in April 2014 and the two girls appeared in propaganda videos after they arrived in Raqqa, fully veiled and enthusing about life under the caliphate. But within six months Ms Kesinovic was desperate to go home, a change of heart ISIS punished by locking her in a house where she was passed round new recruits and multiply raped. When she tried to escape, she was beaten to death with a hammer.[146] This sequence of events had a traumatic impact on Khadiza Sultana: in December 2015, just ten months after she left London, she had a tearful conversation with her sister in which she estimated her own chances of escape as 'zero'. Nothing more was heard of her until the following summer, when her family said that they believed she had been killed in a Russian air strike in May 2016.

Her death was confirmed early in 2019 when another of the girls, Shamima Begum, was recognised in a refugee camp in Syria by a *Times* journalist following the collapse of the caliphate. By then aged nineteen and nine months pregnant, Shamima said she had had two previous babies with her husband, a Dutch fighter, but had lost both to illness and malnutrition. She had heard that her two remaining British friends were alive in recent weeks but did not know what had happened to them. Shamima expressed no regrets about joining ISIS, but said she was tired of life on a battlefield and wanted to come back to the UK.[147] She gave birth to a boy shortly afterwards who later died, aged three weeks, in the camp. The Home Secretary, Sajid Javid, made a controversial decision to strip her of British citizenship. It prompted a row about the treatment of returnees from Syria and Iraq which had not been resolved at the time of writing.

The rapist 'state'

For centuries, the mass rape of women and girls in war was treated as a dirty secret, if it was addressed at all. Comedians made jokes about 'rape and pillage', making light of sexual violence and reflecting the notion that it was an inevitable side effect of conflict – an overspill of testosterone or a means of relieving stress. The mass rape of German women by Soviet troops at the end of the Second World War was not spoken about for decades, neither by the perpetrators nor their victims; soldiers knew perfectly well that their behaviour was unacceptable, something that needed to be covered up on return to civilian life, and they relied on their victims' misplaced sense of shame – and fear of being rejected by husbands and families – to protect them from the consequences.

War-crimes tribunals set up at the end of the war didn't address sexual violence, and there was nothing to stop mass rape happening again in the 1990s, in Europe *and* in Africa. It was a feature of the genocide in Rwanda in 1994, when members of the Hutu majority turned on their Tutsi neighbours, leading to the sexual mutilation, rape and murder of hundreds of thousands of women – not as a side effect of the conflict, but as a deliberate tactic to terrorise and humiliate. But it was the Bosnian war, in which thousands of Muslim women were systematically and repeatedly raped, that finally persuaded the UN Security Council to declare rape in war an international crime. The International Criminal Tribunal for former Yugoslavia (ICTY) subsequently handed down a series of landmark decisions, beginning in 1998 when it recognised rape as 'a powerful tool of war, used to intimidate, persecute and terrorise the enemy'. Not long afterwards, at the trial of three Bosnian Serb army officers who imprisoned Muslim women in so-called 'rape camps' in the eastern town of Foca, the ICTY ruled for the first time that sexual enslavement was a crime against humanity. The court's description of what happened to the women in Foca was explicit:

> Bosnian Serbs gathered Muslim women in detention centres around the town where they were raped by Serb soldiers. Many women were then taken to apartments and hotels run as brothels for Serb soldiers. The judges heard the testimonies of over 20 women regarding repeated acts of rape, gang rape and other kinds of sexual assault and intimidation.
>
> The women also described the way in which they were obliged to perform household chores, were forced to comply with all the demands of their captors, were unable to move freely and were bought and sold like commodities. In short, they lived in conditions of enslavement.[148]

This was a turning point – or so it seemed. It had taken centuries, but the international community had finally reached a point where the specifically sexual damage done to women and girls in war was recognised for what it was – a deliberate tactic, sanctioned by commanders, to reward soldiers and demoralise the enemy.

Over the next few years, the number of convictions for rape in war and sexual enslavement remained low, around thirty by 2011, but it felt as though there had been a sea change in the public perception of soldiers' behaviour towards women; feminists and human-rights activists hoped that the risk of a war-crimes prosecution, and a long prison sentence, would make military leaders think twice in future.

That optimism now seems misplaced, not least because the long-running conflict in Syria has been characterised by war crimes on a vast scale, including the mass rape of women *and* men in the regime's terrible prisons. At the same time, the changing nature of conflict – principally a shift away from violence perpetrated by state actors towards that committed by terrorist groups – has seen an escalation in what the UN still calls gender-based violence (GBV), although it's more accurate to describe it as sex-based. The ideology of organisations such as AQ was implicitly sex-segregated and misogynistic – Mohamed Atta, leader of the 9/11 attackers, famously insisted in his will that his dead body should be washed by a man, and women wouldn't be allowed to attend his funeral – but more recent Islamist groups such as ISIS and Boko Haram, which operates in Nigeria, have weaponised misogyny to attract new followers. While ISIS propagandists were telling vulnerable girls how wonderful life was for women in the caliphate, the message for male foreign fighters was brutally different: come to Syria and get your own sex slave. The UN Security Council put it in more restrained language in a report published in 2015, laying bare the geographical spread of this horrible new tactic. It said:

> The confluence of crises wrought by violent extremism has revealed a shocking trend of sexual violence employed as a tactic of terror by radical groups. Egregious forms of conflict-related sexual violence have been perpetrated by extremist groups in Iraq, Mali, Nigeria, Somalia and the Syrian Arab Republic, including rape, sexual slavery, forced marriage, forced pregnancy and forced abortion, including as a form of religious and ethnic persecution.[149]

The report goes on to say that, far from being incidental, these manifestations of violence against women are 'integrally linked with the strategic objectives, ideology and funding' of terrorist groups. Instead of trying to cover up what they are doing, as armies and militias did in the past, these groups have used the opportunity to rape with impunity and own 'sex slaves' as a powerful 'pull factor'. The UN report says as much:

> [Sexual violence] is used to advance such tactical imperatives as *recruitment*; terrorizing populations into compliance; displacing communities from strategic areas; generating revenue through sex trafficking, the slave trade, ransoms,

looting and the control of natural resources; torture to elicit intelligence; conversion and indoctrination through forced marriage; and to establish, alter or dissolve kinship ties that bind communities. [My italics][150]

Some former fighters, interviewed by researchers on their return from Syria, have freely admitted that the prospect of owning female slaves was one of the lures that drew them to join ISIS in the first place.[151] Siddhartha Dhar, a Muslim convert and bouncy-castle salesman from east London, fled the country while awaiting trial on terrorist offences and has since been accused of rape as well as kidnapping and trafficking girls in Mosul. In chapter five, we saw how ISIS recruited young men with gang connections and records for acquisitive crime, such as theft and armed robbery. But it is clear that it viewed sexual predators, including convicted rapists, as ideal candidates to become foreign fighters and suicide bombers – young men like Ondogo Ahmed, for instance. Ahmed, who was from north London, was only eighteen in 2007 when he was sentenced to eight years in prison for his part in the brutal gang rape of a girl in a flat in Crouch End; as soon as Ahmed was released on licence (unwisely, it might be argued) in 2013, he fled to Syria to join ISIS and was welcomed with open arms, reportedly dying in battle a few weeks later in Homs. Then there was Naa'imur Zakariyah Rahman, a twenty-one-year-old suspected paedophile who was convicted in 2018 of plotting to decapitate the Prime Minister, Theresa May, after bombing the gates of Downing Street; Rahman was caught when he revealed his plans to undercover officers from the FBI and MI5, wrongly believing them to be members of ISIS, but his original arrest was on suspicion of sending indecent images to underage girls, although he was never charged. Nikita Malik, director of the Centre on Radicalisation and Terrorism at the Henry Jackson Society, has suggested that such cases indicate 'a type of terrorism that is sexually motivated, in which individuals with prior records of sexual violence are attracted by the sexual brutality carried out by members of Islamic State.'[152]

ISIS was one of the first terrorist groups to take advantage of the opportunities offered by social media, something that barely existed when AQ gained worldwide notoriety with the 9/11 attacks in 2001. The organisation shamelessly advertised its scorn for equality and human rights, posting pictures of modern-day 'slave markets' in Syria and using its online magazine *Dabiq* to showcase the role played by sexual and domestic violence in its heartlands. 'Slave-girls or prostitutes?' one article asked, arguing that sex with abducted women wasn't rape, while individual members of ISIS boasted about their treatment of captured women and girls from one of Iraq's minority populations, the Yazidis.

Persecution is by no means a new phenomenon for the Yazidis, who have been wrongly characterised as devil worshippers by some Muslims, but the scale of what they have suffered since August 2014, when ISIS fighters overran villages on a plain next to Mount Sinjar in northern Iraq, is heartbreaking.

Estimates of casualties vary but an authoritative report in a medical journal has suggested that 3,100 Yazidis were killed and 6,800, most of them women and girls, were abducted.[153] A UN Commission accused ISIS of genocide, crimes against humanity and war crimes against the Yazidis, focusing in particular on the sexual enslavement of female children and young women:

> Thousands of women and girls, some as young as nine, have been sold in slave markets, or *souk sabaya*, in the Syrian governorates of Raqqah, Aleppo, Homs, Hasakah and Dayr Az-Zawr. ISIS and its fighters hold them both in sexual slavery and in slavery . . . with Yazidi women and girls being constantly sold, gifted and willed between fighters. One woman, who estimated she had been sold 15 times, told the Commission, 'It is hard to remember all those who bought me'.[154]

A teenage Yazidi woman from Kocho, a village near Mount Sinjar, offered a devastating first-hand account of a 'slave market' in a warehouse in Raqqa in a book she published after her escape from an ISIS camp in an oilfield in Syria.[155] Using the pseudonym Farida Khalaf, she described how a Palestinian fighter forced her and other Yazidi girls to line up in front of prospective buyers. One of them, a portly man with a sparse beard, pointed at Farida and demanded to know how old she was. She recalls: 'When he tried to push my jaws apart my heart started thumping like mad. It seemed as if he wanted to check the quality of my teeth. I was reminded of the livestock market in Kocho; this is how the men would check donkeys and cows before buying them.'[156]

This extraordinarily brave young woman was beaten unconscious by the prospective purchaser and sold to a series of different men, including an Azerbaijani fighter who 'bought' her for fifty dollars. Other women were sold for much higher amounts, running into thousands of dollars, and there is no doubt that this form of sex trafficking was a lucrative source of funds for ISIS.

But the telling thing about the accounts of Yazidi women who managed to escape is how rapidly ISIS was able to normalise a culture of sexual violence in the areas it controlled. In January 2016, for instance, a fawning obituary of the ISIS killer Mohammed Emwazi offered an instance of his supposedly generous nature, describing how he passed a woman he'd been given as a sex slave to another fighter who had been injured, 'likewise as a gift'.[157] The inclusion of this anecdote, about two men sharing a captured woman for rape – we don't know her name, age or eventual fate – displayed an almost adolescent pleasure in revealing how completely a young man from north-west London had rejected the values of his home country. There was even a pamphlet, published by something called the Research and Fatwa Department of ISIS, which laid out the conditions in which fighters were allowed to have sex with captive women.[158] Presented as a theological debate, it comprised a series of questions and answers, advising that it was 'permissible' to have sex with a female captive immediately after she was taken prisoner, as long as she was a virgin; with a 'female slave' who hadn't reached puberty, as long as she was physically able to have sex; but not with two sisters or an aunt and niece, and certainly not at the same time. It asserted that female slaves whose master died became part of his estate, to be distributed among relatives along with rest of his property – a circumstance that would have applied to many captive women, given the high attrition rate among ISIS fighters. Despite the dry language, this was nothing less than an exercise in codifying rape, normalising sexual violence in defiance of international law. It had two effects, inviting any and every sexual predator who liked the idea of having female slaves to join ISIS in Syria or Iraq and – just as importantly, I suspect – sticking two fingers up at modern notions of universal human rights. (Its appeal to an out-and-out misogynist like the Manchester bomber, Salman Abedi, should come as no surprise.) ISIS was telling the world it was an organisation for rapists, paedophiles and domestic abusers – and proud of it. And nothing said that more than the behaviour of its leader, Abu Bakr al-Baghdadi, who set an example to his followers by keeping underage Yazidi girls and an American hostage as his personal sex slaves.

Baghdadi was born in Iraq in 1971, although much about his past is obscured by an absence of records and the myths that grow up around such individuals. Even the name we know him by is a nom de guerre, but what's certain is that he is one of the world's most wanted terrorists, with a bounty of $25 million placed on his head by the American government. Baghdadi has been reported killed or badly injured in air strikes on several occasions, only to be heard speaking on audio tapes or providing other indications that he was still alive. Originally a supporter of the Muslim Brotherhood, he formed an Islamist militia after the invasion of Iraq in 2003 and was arrested by the Americans the following year, spending several years in the Camp Bucca detention centre. It isn't clear when Baghdadi was released, a decision that the Americans lived to regret, but in 2010 he was named leader of AQ's Iraqi affiliate, the Islamic State in Iraq (ISI). He regarded the opening of the civil war in Syria as an opportunity to expand his territory, eventually founding ISIS in 2013 and trying – although he failed, as we saw in chapter four – to incorporate AQ's Syrian offshoot, the al-Nusra Front, into his new organisation. AQ recognised ISIS as a deadly rival and disowned it in February 2014, but Baghdadi was undaunted. In July that year, in what was as much a PR stunt as anything else, he made a rare public appearance at the Great Mosque in Mosul and declared himself caliph, or leader, of the world's Muslims. What wasn't public knowledge at the time, although it later became so, was that Baghdadi was a serial rapist, using his position to prey on women and girls captured by ISIS.

Almost a year earlier, in the summer of 2013, fighters from his organisation captured an American aid worker, Kayla Mueller from Arizona, after she had been to visit a hospital run by the

NGO Médecins Sans Frontières in Aleppo. Ms Mueller was held in a house belonging to one of ISIS's middle-ranking figures, a Tunisian known by the nom de guerre Abu Sayyaf, and for a time she was locked in a room with four Yazidi teenagers. The person with day-to-day charge of the prisoners was Abu Sayyaf's wife, Umm Sayyaf, who was later captured in a raid that killed her husband in May 2015. According to an FBI affidavit, Umm Sayyaf acknowledged that she was the women's principal jailer whenever her husband was away. She also admitted knowing that Baghdadi 'owned' Ms Mueller – that she was his sex slave, in other words. The FBI affidavit goes on: 'The captives were at various times handcuffed, held in locked rooms, and given orders on a daily basis with respect to their activities, movements and liberty. While in captivity, Kayla Jean Mueller was sexually abused by Baghdadi, who forced her to have sex with him.'[159]

This account was fleshed out by one of the Yazidi girls, who was only fourteen when she shared a room with Ms Mueller. After her escape from ISIS, she described how Ms Mueller was forced into an Islamic 'marriage' – a euphemism for rape – with Baghdadi, who also raped one of the Yazidi teenagers. The Yazidi girls regarded Ms Mueller as a big sister and were grateful to her for trying to comfort them, but she always returned in tears when Baghdadi took her away. The Americans tried to rescue her on several occasions but she is believed to have died in an air strike in February 2015, after enduring eighteen months of sexual violence and imprisonment. Abu Bakr al-Baghdadi is still believed to be alive, at the time of writing, on the run after creating one of the first terrorist organisations that explicitly put male violence at its core.

The fact that this aspect of contemporary terrorism has been so neglected in mainstream commentary is testament to a wider failure. Like domestic violence, with which it is intertwined, sexual violence has never received the attention it deserves, even in peaceful societies. In war zones, it remains a constant feature but is still swept under the carpet, allowing foolish young men – and some misguided young women, as we have seen in this chapter – to make heroes out of rapists and misogynists. In countries where terrorist organisations like ISIS and al-Shabaab are operating, rape and sexual enslavement are a perpetual threat, making a mockery of their supporters' claims to be fighting against injustice.

This habit of silence is finally being challenged by some very brave women who have survived horrific sexual violence, in defiance of the shame which is so often imposed on rape victims. Very unusually, the 2018 Nobel peace prize acknowl-edged this specific experience of women in war, awarded jointly to Nadia Murad, a Yazidi human-rights activist who now lives in Germany, and Denis Mukwege, a gynaecologist who has treated hundreds of victims of rape in the Democratic Republic of Congo.

Ms Murad has spoken frankly about her experience as a cap-tive of ISIS in 2014, when she endured three months of gang rape, torture and beatings. Dr Mukwege has called on the world to take a tougher line on rape as a weapon of war, describing it as a 'cheap and efficient' species of terror. 'For 15 years I have witnessed mass atrocities committed against women's bodies and I cannot remain with my arms folded because our common humanity calls on us to care for each other,'[160] Dr Mukwege said when the recipients of the prize were announced.

It is a lesson that many commentators should take to heart, not least those historians and experts on terrorism who habit-ually relegate the experience of thousands of raped and abused women to a footnote.

7

Angry White Men

Up to this point, most of the accounts of mass murder and sexual violence in this book have been drawn from the activities of supporters of Islamist organisations such as AQ, AQAP, ISIS, the al-Nusra Front and Boko Haram. That's because such groups, while certainly not having a monopoly on terrorist tactics, have inspired, if not actually directed, most of the fatal attacks on civilians in western Europe, Africa and the Middle East in recent years. It was a different story in the second half of the twentieth when an earlier generation of terrorist organisations were staging bombings, abductions and hijackings.

Terrorism in Northern Ireland had religious affiliations – Catholic in the case of the IRA, Protestant in that of the UDF – but the Basque terrorist organisation ETA was secular and nationalist, as were some of the Palestinian terrorist groups.

In recent years, intelligence agencies across western Europe have become concerned about the rise of various right-wing ideologies, including some that are specifically neo-Nazi, but Islamist organisations have caused the greatest number of civilian casualties in the first two decades of the twenty-first century. They have been behind several terrorist attacks in the US, including 9/11, yet it's essential to point out that most mass killings by a single perpetrator have nothing to do with Islamists.

The US is unique among modern democratic states in having an endemic problem with mass shootings, most of them carried out by individuals who appear to have either a very weak or no known affiliation with terrorist organisations. The vast majority fall into the category of angry white men and they are usually written off as disturbed loners, as though they're entirely disconnected from ideology *and* the culture that produced them. The obvious explanation for the phenomenon of mass murder in the US is the easy availability of guns, especially rapid-fire weapons capable of firing dozens of lethal rounds per minute (imagine how many more people would have died in London if Darren Osborne or Khalid Masood had access to firearms).

The failure of gun control tends to mask the fact that America's weapons culture is an ideology in itself, associated with ideas about the importance of the individual over the state, a right to self-defence which encourages paranoid attitudes to outsiders and a notion of guns as a symbol of manhood. Firearms enthusiasts visit gun fairs up and down the country, browsing the kind of weapons available only to the armed forces in other countries, and they're bombarded with crude messages about the supposedly empowering effect of gun ownership.

The most notorious advertising campaign in the entire history of American gun culture was for the Bushmaster AR-15 assault rifle, consisting of a photograph of this deadly weapon next to the slogan 'Consider your man card reissued'. In answer to the question 'What's a man card?' it explained: 'In a world of rapidly depleting testosterone, the Bushmaster Man Card declares and confirms that you are a Man's Man, the last of a dying breed, with all the rights and privileges duly afforded.' The carbine featured in the campaign was one of the firearms used by Adam Lanza, perpetrator of the Sandy Hook School massacre in December 2012. The Bushmaster campaign was pulled in the wake of that atrocity but other gun manufacturers have promoted a hyper-masculine identity in which the mere act of buying a weapon supposedly turns ordinary men, however insignificant they feel, into warriors. 'His other weapon is an F/A-18' (a fighter jet) was the strapline on an advert for a SIG Sauer machine pistol, the words superimposed on a photograph of a fighter pilot. The Remington gun company suggested, in an advert putting the country's politicians on notice, that purchasers of its rifles were joining an unofficial army: 'Over 5,000,000 sold: the world's largest army ain't in China'. This propaganda is so effective that collecting guns becomes an obsession for some men: Stephen Paddock, perpetrator of the Las Vegas massacre in October 2017, had an arsenal of more than twenty weapons in the hotel room he used as a base for the murders. The constant promotion of gun ownership to disturbed individuals, some of whom we will meet in this chapter, comes close to being a form of radicalisation in itself. The idea that gun culture is apolitical is disproved by the fact that the National Rifle Association, which counts President Donald Trump among its most enthusiastic supporters, is one of the most powerful lobbying organisations in the US.

But there is one more thing, in addition to obsessive gun ownership, that unites the suspicious, resentful men in this chapter – and that's a lethal form of misogyny. Canada is usually regarded as a less dangerous country than its larger neighbour, and it's true that it has lower levels of gun crime than the US. But a vehicle attack in Toronto in 2018, which killed ten people, was the *third* instance of a mass murderer targeting principally female victims in Canada since 1989, when Marc Lépine shot dead fourteen female students at a university in Montreal. In the US, the seat of misogyny is more often than not the family: according to research carried out by the Violence Policy Center, women are much more likely to be killed by a husband, boyfriend or male family member than by someone they don't know. An analysis of American murder victims in 2015 shows that:

— 93 per cent of female victims (1,450 out of 1,551) were murdered by someone they knew.
— *Fourteen times* as many women were murdered by

a man they knew (1,450 victims) than by a male
stranger (101 victims).

— Among victims who knew their killers, 64 per cent
(928 out of 1,450) were wives, partners, ex-wives or
girlfriends of the offenders.[161]

Time and time again, these men turn out to have a prior
history of domestic abuse, often stretching back years and
involving more than one victim; some of the worst examples
are familicides, wiping out more than one generation of the
same family. In the US, one of the most staggering instances
happened in 1982 when a former prison guard, George Banks,
murdered thirteen people in Wilkes-Barre, Pennsylvania; Banks
shot dead three current girlfriends, a step-daughter, an ex-
girlfriend, her mother, her nephew, five of his own children
and a neighbour.

Another study found that there were more than eleven
murder–suicides *each week* in the US during the first six months
of 2017[162] but they're usually treated as a distinct category of
crime, even though some meet the FBI's test for mass murder
or a spree killing (the latter is one which involves outbursts
of violence in several locations). The separation is even odder
when you consider the fact that *over half* of mass murders in
the US include a female relative among the victims, often
beginning with the murder of a partner, ex-partner, mother
or mother-in-law. One of the best-known studies, carried out
by an NGO which lobbies for restrictions on gun ownership,

Everytown for Gun Safety, found that the perpetrator killed an intimate partner or family member in 57 per cent of mass shootings in the US between January 2009 and June 2014.[163] Mass shootings remain rare in the UK but one of the most notorious, the Hungerford massacre in 1987, followed this pattern precisely. The perpetrator, twenty-seven-year-old Michael Ryan, began his rampage with the murder of his mother, Dorothy Ryan, with whom he shared a house, before heading into town and killing fifteen other people and, finally, himself.

The percentage of US mass killings which involve misogyny is actually higher than the statistics on victims suggest. Even in crimes which don't include a female relative among the dead, it often turns out that the perpetrator had a lengthy history of domestic violence. The Pulse nightclub killer, Omar Mateen, although not technically an angry white man, is so similar in this respect to other mass killers that some people have questioned whether he should be regarded as a terrorist at all, despite his declaration of loyalty to ISIS and al-Baghdadi. It has to be said, of course, that the outcome of a terrorist attack and a mass shooting is the same, for the victims and their families, and maintaining rigid distinctions between mass killers and terrorists risks missing the extent to which misogyny is implicated in both sets of crimes.

The angry white men who appear in this chapter were not motivated by ISIS or any other terrorist group but their outbursts of violence had the same lethal effect – and what comes up again and again is the way in which they blame women for their problems. What follows is a summary of some of the most notorious mass killings in recent American history, highlighting the role of domestic violence in their motivation and planning.

Sandy Hook Elementary School, Newtown, Connecticut

The mass shootings at an elementary (primary) school in Connecticut in 2012 were a heart-stopping crime, even in a nation where school killings are not unheard-of events. On Friday, 14 December, a tall, spectrally thin young man called Adam Lanza walked into the school where his mother had once been a volunteer helper, carrying four firearms. Lanza, who was only twenty, used two of the guns to kill twenty children and six adults. He then turned one of the guns on himself, dying from a single shot to his head. Lanza's child victims were six or seven years of age, barely old enough for the survivors to comprehend what had happened to their friends, and the twenty-six murders at the school dominated headlines for months afterwards. That's understandable, given the horror that unfolded at the school, but it obscures an important fact: the massacre was preceded by the murder of Lanza's mother Nancy, fifty-two, whom he killed with four shots to the head as she lay in bed, bringing the number of victims to twenty-seven.

Matricide has been regarded with peculiar horror since time immemorial, playing a prominent role in Greek tragedy –

according to Aeschylus's version of the myth, Orestes is driven mad and pursued by the Furies after he murders his mother, Clytemnestra – but this modern instance has been written out of history. Two days after the massacre, when the then President, Barack Obama, spoke at a vigil for the victims in Newtown, he didn't mention Nancy Lanza at all.[164] As far as Obama was concerned, the victims were 'twenty beautiful children and six remarkable adults', all of whom he named in the course of his speech. The exclusion of Lanza's first victim, the one he knew intimately and had planned to kill for months, is a vivid illustration of the way in which domestic violence disappears from the record.

In the case of Sandy Hook, it has become habitual; in September 2018, while I was finishing this book, I heard the presenter of a Radio 4 documentary mention the six adults and twenty children killed in the massacre, once again ignoring Lanza's mother. No doubt Obama was as shocked as anyone else when he made his speech, so soon after the killings, but the idea that Nancy Lanza shouldn't be mentioned in the same breath as the non-related victims comes close to victim-blaming – something that other commentators were all too ready to do, not least because she owned the guns her son used in the massacre. They also seized on sections of an FBI analysis, published much later, which described Lanza's relationship with his mother as 'a significant challenge and stressor in his life'.[165] Of course it's perfectly possible to read the phrase the other way round, inferring that Nancy Lanza was struggling to cope on her own with a depressed and disturbed young man who was reluctant to leave the house they shared. Most of Lanza's interactions with other people were online, so she may not have known about his obsessive interest in mass killings, especially the Columbine High School shootings, or what the FBI described as an interest in children that 'could be categorized as pedophilia'.[166]

Yet the erasure of Nancy Lanza from the list of her son's victims, disturbing though it is, is not the only way in which public perception of the Newtown massacre has been distorted. Besides his mother, Adam Lanza's adult victims included six dead and two injured at the school – and all eight were women. In a primary school, teachers are very much in loco parentis to their small charges and Lanza may have seen them as mother figures; one of the few adult men on the premises, the janitor Rick Thorne who bravely confronted Lanza, wasn't injured at all.

The Newtown massacre has rightly earned a place as one of the most horrific examples of a school shooting in modern American history, carried out by an angry young man who was obsessed with firearms. But the fact that it began with a lethal act of domestic violence – and the evidence of Adam Lanza's deep-seated misogyny in his choice of adult victims – has barely been acknowledged.

Sutherland Springs, Texas

The First Baptist Church in Sutherland Springs, a rural area of Texas, was packed with people on the morning of Sunday, 5 November 2017. The congregation included the fourteen-year-old daughter of the pastor, Frank Pomeroy, who happened not to be in the church that morning, and a visiting pastor, Bryan Holcombe, who had arrived with several members of his family. Shortly after eleven a.m., a twenty-six-year-old ex-serviceman called Devin Patrick Kelley, who lived in the small town of New Braunfels, around thirty-five miles away, drew up in an SUV and parked near the church door. He cut an alarming figure, dressed in black, wearing a bulletproof vest and carrying a Ruger semi-automatic rifle, and he began firing as soon as he got out of his vehicle. Kelley killed two people in the street, ran inside the church and started shooting indiscriminately, ending his rampage only when everyone in the congregation was dead or injured.

Twenty-three people died inside the church and another in hospital, bringing the number of fatalities to twenty-six, while another twenty were injured. The visiting pastor, Bryan Holcombe, was murdered along with no fewer than eight members of his family. Most of the dead were female: ten women and seven girls, including the resident pastor's teenage daughter. Outside the church, Kelley was confronted by a local man, Stephen Willeford, who happened to be armed with his own semi-automatic weapon. Willeford shot Kelley twice, causing him to drop his rifle, but Kelly returned fire with a handgun and managed to escape in his SUV. Willeford stopped a pick-up truck and persuaded the driver to chase Kelley's vehicle at high speed, calling the police as they went. During the chase, Kelley made calls to his father, telling him he was injured and unlikely to survive, and to his estranged second wife, apologising for the massacre in the church. He then lost control of the SUV, hitting a road sign and careering across a field before coming to a stop and shooting himself in the head.

The clue to the origin of these horrendous events lay in the identity of Kelley's oldest victim, seventy-one-year-old Lula Snow. Ms Snow was a regular worshipper at the First Baptist Church, along with her daughter, Michelle Shields. Ms Shields, who wasn't at the service when Kelley burst in, was the mother of his second wife, Danielle Shields – Kelley's mother-in-law, in other words. He had sent her a series of threatening text messages before the massacre, prompting investigators to suggest that the killings were motivated by a 'domestic situation'[167] – something of an understatement in relation to Kelley.

He turned out to have a long and extremely violent history involving his first and second wives and an ex-girlfriend, along with animal cruelty. In 2012, while Kelley was stationed at a USAF base in New Mexico, he was charged with kicking and choking his first wife, Tessa Kelley, and threatening her with a loaded gun; he was also charged with a savage attack on his stepson, hitting the boy's head so hard that he fractured his skull. The prosecution agreed to drop the weapons charge but Kelley was convicted on two counts of assault, sentenced to twelve months' confinement and demoted in rank; there appears to have been a question about his mental state because he was held for a time at a mental-health facility in New Mexico, from which he briefly escaped. He was recaptured and his bad behaviour continued: a police report recorded that he made death threats against senior officers and tried to smuggle weapons on to an air base. His wife divorced him in 2013 and he was thrown out of the USAF a year later for bad conduct. His convictions for domestic violence should have prevented him from buying and owning firearms but the USAF failed to pass the information on to the federal database used to carry out background checks on would-be weapons purchasers. Kelley was thus able to pass the checks and acquire four guns between 2014 and 2017.

After his discharge from the air force, Kelley went back to New Braunfels, where he moved into a barn next to his parents' house. In the period between his return to Texas and the church massacre, Kelley was repeatedly in trouble with the police. He was accused of attacking women on two occasions, including an incident in 2013 when he was investigated for rape and sexual assault, but neither incident resulted in charges. The following year he married his girlfriend, Danielle Shields, just a couple of months after she accused him of domestic abuse, and the couple moved from Texas to a trailer park in Colorado Springs. They hadn't been there long when Kelley was charged with animal cruelty, after neighbours saw him repeatedly kicking his dog in the head. He pleaded guilty and not long afterwards moved back to his parents' home in New Braunfels, about an hour's drive from where his second wife's family attended church most Sundays. Kelley apparently held his mother-in-law, Michelle Shields, responsible for the break-up of his marriage, and he was looking for her when he stormed into the church. Instead he killed her mother, Lula Snow, and twenty-five other people, including a pregnant woman. A week earlier, this dyed-in-the-wool misogynist posted a photo of the Ruger rifle he would use in the massacre on his Facebook page. The caption read: 'She's a bad bitch'.

Rancho Tehama, California

Nine days after Kelley's attack on the church in Texas, a forty-four-year-old man called Kevin Janson Neal embarked on a spree killing in an impoverished rural community about 130 miles north of Sacramento. Neal shot dead two of his neighbours, Danny Elliott and his mother, Diana Steele, with whom he had a long-running feud, and then stole their truck. He fired wildly at passers-by, hitting and injuring a woman who was in a car with her three sons, before heading for Rancho Tehama Elementary School where Mr Elliott's seven-year-old son was a pupil. Staff heard the shots and had just enough time to go into lockdown before Neal crashed the stolen vehicle into the school gates. Unable to get into the classrooms, he fired almost a hundred rounds before running into a field and shooting into the air, frustrated by his inability to reach the children and their teachers.

Neal then returned to the truck, drove off and crashed into another vehicle, fatally shooting the female driver and wounding her husband. When another driver stopped to help, thinking he'd witnessed a car accident, Neal shot and injured the man, stole his vehicle and used it to chase and kill a fourth victim. A police officer managed to use his patrol car to block Neal's escape and Neal exchanged fire with the police before killing himself with a shot to the head. Four people died in the rampage, which lasted just short of half an hour, and eighteen were injured.

But more horrors were to come: when police entered Neal's home, they found a fifth victim, his wife Barbara Glisan, thirty-eight, whose body was riddled with bullets. Neal had murdered her a day earlier and concealed her body under floorboards at their run-down house, which was barely more than a shack. Neighbours said later they had heard the couple having a noisy argument on the night before the killings. 'We believe that's probably what started this whole event,' said the assistant sheriff, Phil Johnston, highlighting the fact that yet another mass shooting had begun with an act of extreme domestic violence.[168]

It quickly emerged that Neal was an angry, aggressive man, prone to making wild allegations against his neighbours and firing guns outside his home. He was well known to the police, who had been called to incidents twenty-one times in the couple of years before the shootings. Ten months before the murders, he had a violent confrontation with two other neighbours, a woman called Hailey Poland and her mother-in-law; Neal waved around a gun, which he fired several times, stabbed Ms Poland and held the women hostage for a time, a sequence of events that led to his facing charges of assault with a deadly weapon, robbery, false imprisonment and elder abuse. He was granted bail but Ms Poland and her mother-in-law were so terrified that they took out a restraining order a week later, arguing that Neal was unpredictable and unstable. The court did at least make some attempt to deprive him of his firearms, ordering him to hand over his guns, and he surrendered a single pistol. But Neal knew enough about weapons to make a 'ghost' gun at home, a semi-automatic rifle like the ones used in so many mass shootings, and he also managed to get hold of two handguns which weren't legally registered to him.

After the murders, relatives said that Neal had had mental problems for years, and the Tehama County district attorney described him as a 'deranged, paranoid killer'[169]. No one explained why Neal's bail conditions allowed him to go on living next door to people he had already attacked – and no one seemed to have realised, until her body was found under the floorboards, that the person most likely to be at risk from such a violent, unstable man was the woman living with him in his own home.

Virginia Tech

At around seven a.m. on the morning of 16 April 2007, a twenty-three-year-old student began firing at students and lecturers on the campus of Virginia Tech, a university in Blacksburg, Virginia. Like Omar Mateen, Seung-Hui Cho wasn't an angry white man – he was originally from South Korea – but his murders follow the same pattern as the other mass killers in this chapter. His first burst of firing killed two people in a university hall of residence but there was then a gap of more than two hours during which Cho posted a package containing videos, photographs and a rambling 'manifesto' to NBC. He went next to the university's engineering and science building, where he killed another thirty people and injured seventeen before shooting himself in the head. Six more people were hurt when they jumped from upper-floor windows.

In the aftermath of the murders, Cho's history of disturbing behaviour quickly began to emerge. He was withdrawn and reluctant to speak to people he didn't know, introducing himself as 'question mark' instead of giving his name, but on other occasions he launched into obvious fabrications about having a girlfriend who was a supermodel or going on holiday with Vladimir Putin. His written coursework included violent fantasies which worried his lecturers, but the most telling thing in Cho's background was a history of stalking women.

In the autumn of 2005, two female students stopped coming

to a class taught by the distinguished poet Nikki Giovanni because Cho had used his mobile phone to take photographs under their desks. Such behaviour was almost unheard of at the time but it's now known as 'up-skirting', something that became a criminal offence in England and Wales in January 2019. Ms Giovanni was so alarmed that she made a formal request to the head of the English department, Lucinda Roy, asking to have Cho banned from her classes. 'I was willing to resign before I was going to continue with him,' she said after the massacre.[170] Ms Roy offered to tutor Cho herself but his behaviour was so frightening that she agreed a code word with her assistant, telling her to call security if she heard Ms Roy use it.

Cho's aggressive behaviour towards women continued: a female student complained to a student adviser about getting unwanted messages from him, including finding a question mark – the sign Cho sometimes used instead of his name – scrawled on a board near her door. Towards the end of 2005, a second stalking case involving a different student was reported to the police, leading to Cho being interviewed and warned to leave both women alone. He responded by threatening to kill himself, a reaction that foreshadowed the angry self-exculpation in the 'manifesto' he would later send to NBC. He was briefly committed to a mental-health facility near Virginia Tech but was released after a couple of days and allowed to return to the campus.

Despite his lengthening history of voyeurism and stalking, he never faced criminal charges. Less than eighteen months later, he bought two handguns, trained at a public shooting range, five miles from Virginia Tech, and murdered thirty-two people.

Planned Parenthood clinic, Colorado Springs

In photos taken after his arrest, Robert Lewis Dear Jnr looks unkempt, with disordered hair, a bushy beard and staring eyes. A fanatical anti-abortionist, fifty-seven-year-old Dear had just killed three people and injured nine during a siege which lasted five hours at a Planned Parenthood clinic in Colorado Springs, a city close to the Rocky Mountains in Colorado.

Dear tried to force his way into the clinic on a snowy Friday morning, 27 November 2015, but was stopped by staff who heard shots and managed to lock a security door. Unable to get inside, he shot dead one of the first police officers to arrive at the scene, an army veteran who tried to run inside to warn patients that a shooter was on the loose, and a woman who had gone to the clinic to support a friend. Five other police officers were among the injured.

Dear was reclusive, possibly even a survivalist, having lived in a series of isolated trailers including a shack in North Carolina which had no electricity or running water. About a year before the shootings, he bought a five-acre plot of land in a rural area to the west of Colorado Springs and moved into a camper van with his girlfriend. Like many mass killers, he was obsessed with guns, using four semi-automatic rifles to attack the Planned Parenthood clinic, but police also found an arsenal of weapons – two other rifles, a shotgun, two handguns, a hatchet and several knives – in his truck, along with home-made body armour.

He was an evangelical Christian but he wasn't overly concerned with the church's teaching on marriage and fidelity, at one point joining a dating site where he wrote that he was looking for a 'discreet' relationship and was interested in sado-masochistic sex. He railed against abortion, telling one of his ex-wives he had superglued the locks of an abortion clinic in Charleston, South Carolina, many years before the Colorado Springs attack. After his arrest, he repeated an entirely false allegation, circulated in videos made by American anti-abortion activists, that Planned Parenthood clinics were selling 'baby parts';[171] he also claimed that the attack had 'saved lives of other unborn foetuses' and apparently believed that he would be thanked at the gates of heaven by aborted foetuses.

Dear was charged with 179 offences, including three counts of murder, and made no attempt to deny what he had done; appearing in court a couple of weeks after the murders, he shouted that he was guilty, didn't want a trial and described himself as 'a warrior for the babies'.[172] In a highly controversial move, the judge ruled that Dear was unfit to stand trial, a decision that has since been confirmed by other judges on several occasions. He was sent to a mental-health facility, an outcome some critics regard as by no means the first occasion on which he escaped justice.

Dear's history turned out to include a catalogue of violence against women, including domestic abuse, stalking and an arrest on suspicion of rape. He was first accused of domestic violence by his second wife, who claimed he was a problem gambler with a foul temper who beat her up *and* had children with two other women (one of them, bizarrely, his first ex-wife) while they were married. She didn't want to press charges but by the time she filed for divorce in 1993, Dear had been accused of rape by another woman. She said that Dear spotted her in the store where she worked, pestered her for a date and finally turned up at her apartment, where he raped her at knifepoint.[173] She went to the police but a key witness refused to testify and the case was dropped. Dear went on to marry again and his third wife accused him of domestic violence in 1997, telling the police he had locked her out of the house and pushed her out of a window when she tried to climb back in. She said she wanted them to record the incident but declined to press charges, and the marriage ended three years later.

Dear continued to pester women: in 2002, a female neighbour told the police he had made unwanted advances and spied on her from bushes outside her house. He was arrested on 'peeping Tom' charges which were later dropped, for reasons that are unclear, and a few months later another neighbour accused Dear of shooting his dog in the head. He was cleared of two counts of animal cruelty, despite telling a sheriff's deputy that his neighbour 'was lucky that it was only a pellet that hit the dog and not a bigger round'.[174]

Dear is a physically imposing man, thickset and six foot three, who frightened many people he came into contact with, from intimate partners to neighbours who reported him to the police on a number of occasions. The woman who accused him of rape never got over it, according to her husband, and spent the rest of her life (she died in 2007) worrying that Dear would come back and attack her again.[175] Yet his record completely failed to reflect the extent of his offending against women, consisting solely of convictions for driving offences. Victims of domestic violence are sometimes reluctant to press charges, for understandable reasons, but Dear's wives were far from being the only women who complained about his behaviour. And nothing says more about the misogyny of this vicious, controlling man with a liking for sadomasochistic sex than his choice of target: a clinic that offers advice to women who want autonomy over their own bodies.

Isla Vista, California

As we've seen earlier in this book, teenage boys who carry out school shootings often turn out to have idolised the perpetrators of the Columbine High School massacre. A more recent mass killer, twenty-two-year-old Elliot Rodger, has been claimed as one of the inspirations of the overtly misogynistic 'incel' (involuntary celibate) movement, a rather grand term for a group of angry young men who encourage each other's grievances towards women via social-media sites. 'Incels' have a straightforward beef with the modern world, complaining that modern women are inexplicably neglecting their duty to have sex with any man who requires it. Their hero, Rodger, was a college dropout from a middle-class background – his British father and Chinese-Malaysian mother both worked in the film industry – who turned into a brutal spree killer and attacked his victims with knives, handguns and a car. The reason 'incels' like him so much is that he left behind a mass of self-aggrandising material, including videos and a rambling 'manifesto' in which he complained in excruciating detail about women who didn't want to have sex with him. It's become a reference point for other misogynists, who seem happy to overlook both the fact that he was responsible for a bloodbath *and* his racially-fuelled resentment towards other men.

The murders began in Isla Vista, near the campus of the University of California, Santa Barbara, on the evening of Friday, 23 May 2014. Rodger's first victims were two male students he shared an apartment with, whom he stabbed to death along with one of their friends who happened to have come round to see them. Leaving a scene of carnage in the flat, Rodger calmly set off to visit a Starbucks, where he bought a coffee before returning to his car and using his laptop to upload a video pompously entitled 'Elliot Rodger's Retribution'. At the same time, he emailed his 'manifesto' to a number of recipients, including his parents. As soon as he saw the email, Rodger's father, Peter, was so alarmed that he set off for Isla Vista, but it was already too late; he heard breaking news of the massacre on the car radio while he was on his way.

After uploading the video, Rodger had driven to a women's dormitory in search of female victims, shooting three young women who happened to be outside the building and killing two of them. Returning to his car, he shot and killed another man and drove around the area, firing randomly at passers-by. He used his vehicle as a weapon, hitting and injuring several people, exchanged fire with police and was shot in the left hip before crashing his car. He was finally found dead at the wheel, having killed himself with a shot to the head. In all, over a period of several hours, Rodger murdered six people and injured thirteen, including seven who were struck by his car. Forensic reports revealed the brutality of the attacks, with one of his first male victims being stabbed almost a hundred times. The two women killed by Rodger outside the dormitory were shot seven and eight times respectively.

Rodger's 'manifesto' was frank about his belief that he would never lose his virginity, his envy of men who had girlfriends and his hatred of women solely because they weren't attracted to him. Written in the form of an autobiography, it listed one grievance after another, including his anger towards his parents for not being as wealthy as he would have liked them to be. In a hate-filled passage about the year he reached the age of seventeen, Rodger claimed it was the moment his life took 'a dark turn' and he began to fantasise about torturing the young couples he saw around him in California. He wrote:

> I will destroy all women because I can never have them. I will make them suffer for rejecting me. I will arm myself with deadly weapons and wage a war against *all women and the men they are attracted to*. And I will slaughter them like the animals they are. If they won't accept me among them, then they are my enemies. They showed me no mercy, and in turn I will show them no mercy. The prospect will be so sweet, and justice will ultimately be served. [My italics][176]

Much has been written about Rodger's sense of entitlement and its relation to his underlying insecurity. What hasn't received so much attention is the racial element of his grievances, evident in his obsession with fair-haired women and his confused feelings about the fact that he was mixed-race. Recalling an incident at a party, he wrote:

> I came across this Asian guy who was talking to a white girl. The sight of that filled me with rage. I always felt as if white girls thought less of me because I was half-Asian, but then I see this white girl at the party talking to a full-blooded Asian guy. I never had that kind of attention from a white girl! And white girls are the only girls I'm

attracted to, especially the blondes. How could an ugly Asian attract the attention of a white girl, while a beautiful Eurasian like myself never had any attention from them? I thought with rage.[177]

Rodger's misogyny fuelled his envy and hatred of other young men, something evident in his choice of initial victims – his flatmates Weihan Wang and Cheng Yuan Hong, and their friend George Chen – who were all of Chinese heritage.

The 'Retribution' video is full of childish attempts to boost his self-esteem, including passages in which Rodger describes himself as 'magnificent', but it all rings rather hollow. 'I don't know why you girls hate me so much,' he says plaintively at the end of the video, revealing a chasm in his understanding of human nature. In an anguished TV interview a few weeks after the killings, Peter Rodger described his son as unusually shy but said he had missed the fact that the boy was 'very mentally ill'. It may well be that an undiagnosed mental illness played a part in Elliot Rodger's rampage but it hasn't prevented his rants striking a chord with other angry young men. They refer to him in online discussions as 'the ideal magnificent gentleman' or 'Saint Elliot', even expressing a wish in one instance to talk to him about 'the putrid nature of the sluts we so despise'.[178]

The existence of this unpleasant cult wasn't widely known until it was revealed that the suspect in the 2018 Toronto vehicle attack, Alek Minassian, then twenty-five, had made no secret of his admiration for Rodger. Minassian, who is awaiting trial at the time of writing, is alleged to have left a post on Facebook mentioning the Isla Vista killer by name and mocking the couples they both despised: 'The Incel Rebellion has already begun! We will overthrow all the Chads and Stacys! All hail the Supreme Gentleman Elliot Rodger!'[179] Minassian is accused of driving a hired van onto a crowded pavement, killing eight women and two men; the female fatalities in this overtly misogynistic attack included an eighty-year-old woman, a Sri Lankan single mother, a student and an investment banker. Horrifying in itself, the Toronto incident also signalled the risk of copycat attacks by adherents of what appears to be a growing cult, just as the Columbine massacre has been referenced by a whole series of school shooters.

Santa Fe High School, Texas

Shortly before eight a.m. on Friday, 18 May 2018, a teenage boy opened fire in an art class at a school in Texas. The suspect, who was wearing a black trench coat like the ones worn by the Columbine killers, used a Remington shotgun and a revolver legally owned by his father to murder eight students and two teachers, while another thirteen people were injured. Police said that Dimitrios Pagourtzis, a seventeen-year-old pupil at the school, had planned the shooting in some detail, writing about it in a diary, on his computer and a mobile phone. They said he had intended to end the incident by killing himself, but lost his nerve and gave himself up instead. A local judge revealed that Pagourtzis had tried to make a home-made bomb using CO_2 canisters, nails, a pressure cooker and an alarm clock, but it failed to work. In a chilling insight into his yearning for publicity, Pagourtzis said in an affidavit after his arrest that he had allowed students he liked to live 'so he could have his story told'[180].

His Facebook page, which was deleted after the massacre, showed a T-shirt bearing the phrase 'Born to Kill' and an image of an Iron Cross pinned to a trench coat, but very little in the way of warning signs. Then the distraught mother of one of the murdered students, sixteen-year-old Shana Fisher, posted a message on her own Facebook page. In a horribly familiar story, Sadie Rodriguez claimed that her daughter had endured 'four months of problems from this boy'. Pagourtzis 'kept making advances on her and she repeatedly told him no,' Ms Rodriguez wrote; instead of backing off, Pagourtzis got 'more aggressive'. In interviews with the press, she elaborated on what she'd said in the post, recalling that Pagourtzis had previously gone out with one of Shana's friends before he turned his attention to her. 'She wanted nothing to do with him,' Ms Rodriguez said, and then she added a telling detail: just a week before the killings, Shana got so fed up with Pagourtzis that she 'stood up to him' in front of the class, publicly embarrassing him.[181] She believed that her daughter was the first person killed by Pagourtzis, who was charged with ten capital offences of murder despite the fact that the US Supreme Court banned the death penalty for juvenile offenders in 2005. He is awaiting trial at the time of writing.

Harvest music festival, Las Vegas

In the final week of September 2017, a man called Stephen Craig Paddock booked a set of rooms on the thirty-second floor of a hotel in Las Vegas. It offered a panoramic view of an outdoor area where music festivals were held, which was why Paddock wanted that particular suite. His luggage contained a staggering arsenal of weapons, including fourteen semi-automatic rifles which had been modified to fire as fully-automatic weapons, and a vast quantity of ammunition. On the evening of Sunday, 1 October, when more than 20,000 people had gathered for the Harvest country music festival, Paddock opened fire on the audience from his hotel room. Over the next ten minutes, he killed fifty-eight people and injured more than 400; almost as many were hurt as people tried to flee from the festival site, bringing the number of injured to 851. The massacre ended when police arrived and blew open the door to Paddock's hotel suite, which he had screwed shut to delay entry. They found him on the floor, dead from a shot to the head.

Over the next few days, as heart-breaking stories emerged of concert-goers desperately trying to save injured friends and complete strangers, Paddock's history came under minute exam-ination. He was sixty-four, a retired accountant who had built up a successful property empire, and hence much older than the usual run of men who set out to commit mass murder. Origi-nally from the Midwest, he led a restless life, living in Texas and California before retiring to Florida and then finally settling in Nevada in 2016. He had been married twice but at the time of the massacre he was living in the small town of Mesquite, about eighty miles from Las Vegas, with his long-standing Filipina girl-friend, sixty-two-year-old Marilou Danley. There are a number of casinos in Mesquite and Paddock had become an inveterate gambler in his later years, meeting Ms Danley when she was working at a casino in Reno. According to the Las Vegas police, Paddock had lost a 'significant amount' of money in the years before the murders, although he had managed to pay off his gambling debts.[182] In the weeks before the shootings, he told Ms Danley he had wired $100,000 to the Philippines and sent her to collect it, saying it was to help her buy a house for her family. She arrived back from Manila a couple of days after the shootings, genuinely shocked and insisting that she had known nothing about Paddock's plans. Investigators suspected that he deliberately sent her to Manila to avoid suspicion falling on her in the aftermath of the massacre.

None of this explained why Paddock decided to murder so many total strangers. Documents released in 2018 included witness statements from a couple of people who claimed they had heard him repeat right-wing conspiracy theories, but the

Las Vegas police said they were no closer to establishing his motive. At the same time, a disturbing picture of his character and, in particular, his behaviour towards women quickly began to emerge. His younger brother, Eric Paddock, described him as 'the king of micro-aggression', claiming that he would light a cigar and blow smoke into the faces of people who annoyed him, even though he didn't actually smoke.[183] He was arrogant and controlling, according to staff in a Starbucks in Mesquite who recognised Paddock as a regular customer and claimed that he often verbally abused Ms Danley in front of them. They recalled that Paddock refused to allow Ms Danley to use his casino card, which collects credits from electronic gambling machines, to pay for her coffee, saying, 'You don't need my casino card for this. I'm paying for your drink, just like I'm paying for you'.[184] But the most startling testimony came from a woman who worked for a time as a prostitute in Las Vegas, who claimed that Paddock had paid her up to $7,500 a night for sex – including acting out rape fantasies. We've seen in previous chapters that predators have a sixth sense when it comes to vulnerability, and Paddock met the woman when she had just left an abusive relationship and was struggling to survive. He told her he wanted to help and they met in Las Vegas on nine occasions between November 2015 and June 2016, but the reality was rather different. She said: 'We would go to the casinos together and he would spend hours drinking and gambling. But when he would have a winning streak, we would go back and have really aggressive and violent sex.'[185]

The woman showed reporters text messages that appeared to have been sent from Paddock's phone, including one which mentioned tying her up as she 'scream[ed] for help'. Another referred to his father, whom he claimed to hold responsible for his bad behaviour. 'I didn't have anything really to do with him but the bad streak is in my blood. I was born bad,' he wrote in one.

There is no such thing as being 'born bad' but Paddock's family history *was* unusual: his father, Benjamin Paddock, was an escaped bank robber who spent many years on the FBI's 'most wanted' list. Having an absent father is high on the list of ACEs, especially when the cause is something as dramatic as a lengthy prison sentence, but Paddock most certainly *did* know his father – he was seven years old when Benjamin Paddock was convicted of a catalogue of crimes, including fraud and bank robberies. The family lived in a ranch-style house in Tucson, Arizona, and it's telling that the elder Paddock fancied himself as a role model for boys, volunteering to mentor troubled youths despite his already extensive criminal record. His legitimate jobs included running a service station and a nightclub, and there's no reason to think he didn't have an influence on Stephen, who was the eldest of his four sons.

Benjamin Paddock was a big man – an FBI description recorded that he was six foot four and weighed more than seventeen stone – and he must have been a terrifying sight when he burst into banks and threatened the staff with a gun, but he showed no remorse when he underwent a psychiatric assessment in 1960. According to the report, he was moody and volatile, boasting that he was a 'genius' and then describing himself as a 'loser' moments later.[186] The psychiatrist concluded that he had a 'sociopathic personality', and the elder Paddock was convicted and sent to prison for twenty years. His sons were told he was dead but discovered the truth and visited him in jail – until, that is, he managed to escape and spent the best part of the next decade on the run. An FBI 'wanted' poster warned that Benjamin Paddock had been 'diagnosed as psychopathic, [and] has carried firearms in commission of bank robberies. He reportedly has suicidal tendencies and should be considered armed and very dangerous'[187]. Most of those things would later turn out to be true of his eldest son, who achieved a notoriety of sorts as the deadliest lone gunman in modern American history.

Capital Gazette, Annapolis, Maryland

In July 2011, Eric Hartley, a reporter with a local newspaper called the *Capital Gazette* in Annapolis, the capital city of Maryland, covered a routine court case. The defendant, thirty-one-year-old Jarrod Warren Ramos, was accused of stalking a woman he knew from high school after reconnecting with her via Facebook. At the time, cyberstalking was still a novelty and Mr Hartley's article in the *Capital Gazette* appeared under a headline – 'Jarrod wants to be your friend' – which echoed the language of a 'friend' request on Facebook. Ramos had initially asked the woman for help but quickly turned hostile, bombarding her with abusive messages and ignoring her requests to leave her alone. He had a degree in computer engineering and knew his way around the Internet, finding out where she worked and trying to get her sacked from her job as well as accusing her of drinking too much and urging her to kill herself. It was a sustained campaign of bullying and abuse – 'the worst case of harassment and stalking I have ever encountered'[188], according to her lawyer – and went on for more than a year before Ramos pleaded guilty to harassment. Despite the seriousness of the offence, he was sentenced to probation and counselling rather than any time in prison.

Everything in Mr Hartley's account of the court proceedings was true but Ramos was enraged by his exposure as a stalker in the newspaper. He was determined to get revenge, embarking on a vendetta against just about everyone involved in the case, including the victim, her lawyer, the judge who heard the case and the staff of the *Capital Gazette*. He contacted the victim, insisting that she hand over material which would help him in a defamation case against the newspaper, and harassed her lawyer when he tried to shield her from Ramos's demands. The defamation case never had a hope of success but it was part of a wider campaign that escalated to death threats against Mr Hartley and the then editor and publisher of the *Capital Gazette*, Thomas Marquardt. He reported the threats to the police, telling the paper's lawyers he was worried that Ramos might 'come in and shoot us', but the police weren't convinced Ramos was serious.

His obsessive hatred of the media by now extended far beyond the staff of the *Capital Gazette*, latching on to stories about journalists being murdered. He eagerly followed reports of the deaths of foreign correspondents, including the murders of James Foley and Steven Sotloff by ISIS, and posted material about the massacre at the *Charlie Hebdo* office in Paris, including a digitally altered image of one of the paper's staff with a bullet hole in his head. But he never forgot his original grudge against the *Capital Gazette,* tweeting a death threat against Mr Hartley and his editor shortly afterwards.

On Thursday, 28 June 2018, almost seven years after Ramos first appeared in court on the harassment charge, he sent a flurry of threatening letters to various recipients, including one of the judges involved in his unsuccessful attempt to sue for libel. Later that day, he is alleged to have blocked the rear exit of the *Capital Gazette* office in Annapolis and forced his way inside, armed with a pump-action shotgun he had been able to buy legally, despite his criminal record. As staff tried to hide behind filing cabinets and tweeted desperate messages about a shooter in the office, four journalists and a sales assistant were killed, while several other people were injured. (Mr Hartley, fortunately for him, wasn't among the fatalities.) Police rushed to the newspaper office, found Ramos hiding under a desk and took him into custody. He was charged with twenty-three offences, including five murders, and his lawyers indicated at his first court appearance that they were considering a plea that their client was not responsible by reason of insanity. He is awaiting trial at the time of writing.

Harassment via the Internet is a nasty crime, carried out by bullies who think they can get away with it, often against female targets. Ramos chose a victim, a woman he knew slightly from school and didn't consider able to stand up to him, and set about making her life hell. When he was prosecuted, he couldn't bear the shame of public exposure, refusing to leave the woman alone and drawing even more attention to himself. Inevitably, there are occasions when the work of journalists dents the egos of fragile men and Ramos fixed on the staff of the *Capital Gazette* as scapegoats, repeating a pattern we have seen many times in this book. With hindsight, the gravity and persistence of his original offence – not a one-off threat but a campaign of stalking that caused intense fear and anguish – doesn't seem to have been taken into account when police officers were faced with the possibility of escalation. It is clear from this sequence of events that Ramos started out as an angry misogynist, pursuing his female victim in the supposed safety of cyberspace, but he has ended up as the chief suspect in the worst attack on journalists in American history.

Marjory Stoneman Douglas High School, Parkland, Florida

This section of the book ends with the Marjory Stoneman Douglas High School shootings for two reasons: the suspect's lengthy history of domestic violence and the fact that the massacre marked a watershed, inspiring teenage survivors to launch a powerful campaign for more effective gun control. They lobbied local politicians, persuading the Governor of Florida, Rick Scott, to raise the minimum age for buying firearms in the state from eighteen to twenty-one – a small but significant step towards restricting gun ownership – and organised a 'march for our lives' in Washington which was attended by hundreds of thousands of people. Emma González, an eighteen-year-old survivor, read out the names of her murdered classmates and described all the things they wouldn't be able to do because their lives had been cut short. She and other leaders of the #NeverAgain movement appeared on the cover of *Time* magazine, capturing the public imagination and putting the National Rifle Association on the back foot. President Donald Trump, usually so voluble on Twitter, spent the day of the march at one of his golf clubs in Florida and made no comment on it.

The Parkland massacre was the deadliest high-school attack in the US since the Columbine shootings. The attack began on the afternoon of Valentine's day in 2018, when a nineteen-year-old man allegedly walked into his old school, wearing body armour and armed with a semi-automatic weapon. Over the next six minutes, he is said to have killed or fatally wounded seventeen people, two of whom died later in hospital. The dead included three teachers and fourteen students, some as young as fourteen, while another seventeen people were injured. After the shootings, survivors described extraordinary stories of heroism and self-sacrifice, revealing how teachers and students used their bodies to block doors in order to save others. A report from the sheriff's office said that the suspect, Nikolas Cruz, had confessed and told police officers that he 'began shooting students that he saw in the hallways and on school grounds'.[189] He was charged with 34 counts of premeditated murder and attempted murder, and is awaiting trial at the time of writing.

Nikolas had left the school following accusations of stalking and racial abuse, while his mother had been calling the police – and pleading for help with her difficult, periodically violent son – for years before the shootings. He and his half-brother had been adopted by Lynda and Roger Cruz, a couple who were originally from Long Island, New York, but moved to Parkland, Florida, to raise their family. Mr and Mrs Cruz were older than most adoptive parents but they offered the boys a second chance; their biological mother, who had a lengthy criminal record and a history of drug abuse, gave Nikolas up for adoption at birth and later allowed the couple to adopt his younger half-brother, Zachary. Roger Cruz died suddenly at the age of sixty-seven, when Nikolas was six, leaving his wife to look after the brothers on her own until she died of pneumonia, aged sixty-eight, just three months before the massacre.

According to records released after the shootings, Mrs Cruz had struggled to cope with Nikolas's violent behaviour, repeatedly making emergency calls throughout the decade before the massacre. Police logs show she made more than thirty calls, logged under a variety of headings including 'child/elderly abuse', 'domestic disturbance' and 'mentally ill person'. Some of the calls related to fights between the brothers but police records revealed that Nikolas verbally and physically abused his mother, calling her a 'useless bitch' and throwing furniture and other objects[190]. Neighbours reported that he liked hurting animals, shooting at chickens and squirrels with an air gun, and his social media posts included photographs of small animals he claimed to have killed. His online accounts revealed an obsession with firearms and he boasted, five months before the massacre, that he wanted to be 'a professional school shooter'[191]. There were also reports of self-harming and an apparent suicide attempt – a school counsellor reported that Nikolas tried to kill himself by drinking petrol – but psychiatrists and therapists disagreed about diagnosis and treatment. Bizarrely, in light of the fact that his younger half-brother is mixed-race, Nikolas frequently expressed racist views in a private Instagram group, railing against Jews, black people and immigrants.

In 2016, having abused his own mother for years without ever being held to account by the criminal justice system, Nikolas started to mistreat girls his own age. He acquired a girlfriend at Marjory Stoneman Douglas, but the relationship didn't last long because the girl was scared of him. After she finished it, Nikolas began to stalk her, alarming her friends so much that they took turns to walk her to the bus stop after school and made sure she was never alone with him. When the girl started a new relationship, Nikolas turned his attention to her boyfriend, physically attacking him on two occasions and racially abusing him in texts (the boy came from a Hispanic family). By January 2017, teachers and counsellors were so concerned about his behaviour that they recommended a transfer to a small school with mental health services – but he didn't turn up.

Despite this disturbing history, background checks on customers seeking to buy guns are so narrow that there was nothing to stop Nikolas, still only aged eighteen, buying an AR-15-type assault rifle in February that year. Nine months later, his adoptive mother died and he moved in with friends, taking his rifle and several other guns with him. Three months after *that*, this unstable young man with a jaw-dropping history of domestic violence is alleged to have walked back into his old school, opened fire – and prompted the biggest protest movement against uncontrolled gun ownership the US has ever seen.

Summary

The link in this chapter between misogyny and public acts of slaughter is astonishing. Two of the men, Adam Lanza and Kevin Neal, murdered close female relatives before embarking on massacres. Another, Devin Kelley, was hoping to kill his mother-in-law when he started firing in a church in Texas. Nikolas Cruz subjected his adoptive mother to a decade of abuse *and* stalked an ex-girlfriend before he is alleged to have carried out a school shooting. Two other stalkers - Jarrod Ramos and Seung-Hui Cho – used modern technology to harass women they knew from school and college. Elliot Rodger, a pathologically insecure and self-obsessed misogynist, has become a hero for some angry young men who don't have instant access to sex whenever they want it.

At least two of the killers in this chapter had sadomasochistic fantasies about women. Stephen Paddock was wealthy enough to pay vulnerable women to allow him to act them out, avoiding unwanted attention from the law. Robert Dear Jnr looked for 'discreet' partners – presumably he meant women who wouldn't report him for beating them up – on dating sites and was arrested on suspicion of rape, although the case was dropped. Dear's history is remarkable both for the number of women he abused *and* as an example of the dire consequences of failing to prosecute men for domestic and sexual violence.

The same failure comes up time and time again, suggesting that police and prosecutors lack the will or the competence to get convictions – and don't understand that violence in the home may be an early warning sign of violent intentions towards strangers. It is bad enough that this happens in countries like the UK where many women feel they can't rely on the police to protect them against angry and unstable family members, let alone sexual predators. But it is nothing short of catastrophic in the US, where convictions for rape and *some* – though by no means all – forms of domestic violence are among the few obstacles to the easy purchase of semi-automatic weapons. There are significant gaps in the legislation: federal law designed to prevent domestic abusers buying firearms applies only to men who beat up wives or women with whom they have a child. Some of the most common types of abuse – stalking, for example, or violence against a mother – *aren't* covered by federal law, leaving it to individual states to prevent access to guns by convicted stalkers.

Even when a man has a relevant conviction, the information isn't always recorded or shared in the proper manner, a point demonstrated by the failure of the USAF to inform the federal authorities about Devin Kelley's convictions for brutal assaults on his first wife and stepson. The fact remains that, had Kelley's history been shared with the federal database, he wouldn't have been allowed to purchase the weapons he used in the Sutherland Springs shooting – and twenty-six people, including the fourteen-year-old daughter of the church pastor, might still be alive today. Likewise, had Dear been convicted of rape or beating up his ex-wives, he wouldn't have been able to amass the arsenal of firearms he used in the Colorado Springs attack, potentially saving the lives of the three strangers he murdered.

8

Terrorism Begins at Home

'Everyday' male violence is invisible

I have been writing about male violence for decades. I first addressed it in my book *Misogynies*, published in 1989 and still in print, which was inspired (if that's the right word) by my experience of covering the 'Yorkshire Ripper' murders as a young reporter. Vastly outnumbered by male detectives and crime reporters, I was shocked to the core by the casual sexism I encountered. While the men laughed and joked with each other at press conferences, I thought I could easily become the next victim of a killer who so obviously hated women. While they behaved as though they were looking for a monster, something between a pantomime villain and Jack the Ripper, I thought they couldn't find him because he wasn't that different – on the surface, at least – from other men who thought some of the victims 'deserved' what had happened to them. Sometimes I couldn't believe what I was hearing, such as the senior member of the Ripper squad who casually observed that the killer had begun to target 'innocent girls' instead of prostitutes, demonstrating that he was now – though not, presumably, before – in urgent need of medical attention. Peter Sutcliffe, a lorry driver from Bradford whom none of us would have looked twice at if we passed him on the street, was eventually convicted of murdering thirteen women and trying to kill another seven, although the final toll of victims was almost certainly higher.

In a precursor to the arguments I'm making in this book, I pointed out in *Misogynies* that Sutcliffe had grown up with extreme domestic violence, terrorised (along with his mother) by his violent, drunken father. The term 'ACEs', which I've used several times in these pages, hadn't been invented in the 1970s and while Sutcliffe's experience would no doubt score pretty high, nothing that happened to him as a child goes anywhere near excusing his terrible violence. What my experience of reporting the murders *did* do was open my eyes to a vein of misogyny I'd been aware of in literary and popular culture, without ever realising how deep and dangerous it was. The casual way crime reporters and cops talked about some of the victims made me think about something I hadn't previously put into words, which was the normalisation of male violence. Evidently some of it didn't count, if it was against the 'wrong' sort of woman, and there were lots of those: poor women who sold sex for a living, 'nagging' wives or young women who changed their minds about having sex at the last moment. I mean, you can't really call that rape, can you?

I began to see that this was why the Yorkshire Ripper had to be separated off from other men, placed in an entirely different category so they didn't have to think too much about their own behaviour; it's only possible to see men like Sutcliffe as the great exception if you ignore, tolerate or explain away most of the male violence that's going on around us all the time.

That process of diminishing male violence is still happening, with dire implications for the subject of this book. If anything, the denial of sexual *and* domestic violence has got worse, ensuring that most perpetrators never get the criminal records they deserve. The excuses and euphemisms are endless: just a slap, a bit of rough sex, a misunderstanding, even the infamous assertion by a former MP, George Galloway, that women don't need to be asked for consent to sex prior to every 'insertion'. Violent men are *still* telling their partners they can't help losing their tempers because they're jealous and can't bear to see them talking to other men, as if giving someone a black eye is evidence of passion. In the US, in an era of populist politics which reached its nadir with the election to President of a man accused of serial assaults on women, the practice of erasure has happened in plain sight.

During the run-up to the election in 2016, many people thought that Donald Trump was finished when a video emerged in which he bragged about forcing himself on women.

'Grab them by the pussy. You can do anything,' he boasted on what became known as the 'Access Hollywood' tape, made just over a decade earlier when he was still a reality-TV presenter. Many women, myself included, pointed out that grabbing a woman's genitals constitutes sexual assault, and the Republican candidate for the country's highest office had just admitted to being a sexual predator. Not at all, said Trump's supporters, dismissing it with that well-worn phrase 'locker-room banter'. A few weeks later, millions of voters had no qualms about putting a self-confessed sexual predator into the White House.

Trump had previously been accused of rape in his first wife's divorce petition, a document that remained in the public domain even after she retracted the allegation as part of her divorce settlement, but that didn't trouble his supporters either. The new President quickly set about importing a culture of open misogyny into the highest levels of government, looking like a sullen schoolboy as he tried to avoid shaking hands with one of the world's most powerful women, Angela Merkel. His election emboldened opponents of abortion, who proposed new laws restricting access to terminations in one state after another. In the most extreme example, a bill attempting to criminalise abortion in Ohio was couched in such restrictive terms that it would have the effect, if passed, of exposing women who had terminations to charges of murder – and even the death penalty.[192]

The claim that women lie about male violence is central to Trump's view of the world and when a psychology professor,

Christine Blasey Ford, accused his nominee to fill a vacancy on the Supreme Court of attempted rape, he mocked her in front of cheering supporters at a campaign rally in Mississippi. In an article in the *Atlantic*, Adam Serwer forensically identified what Trump was doing when he encouraged his supporters to laugh at Dr Ford. He wrote:

> Even those who believe that Ford fabricated her account, or was mistaken in its details, can see that the president's mocking of her testimony *renders all sexual-assault survivors collateral damage*. Anyone afraid of coming forward, afraid that she would not be believed, can now look to the president to see her fears realized. Once malice is embraced as a virtue, it is impossible to contain. [My italics][193]

Trump was, in effect, warning women that they would be publicly shamed if they dared to accuse powerful men of sexual or domestic violence. The episode was revealing for other reasons as well: Trump's nominee, Brett Kavanaugh, raged and spat abuse, exposing the assumptions of a privileged, entitled man who couldn't believe he was having to answer questions about his past behaviour. Kavanaugh claimed that his entire life had been ruined but the FBI was given just *six days* to investigate Dr Ford's allegations, and he was confirmed by a vote of the Senate just over a week later.

Around the same time, one of the most prestigious publications in the US, the *New York Review of Books*, published a long, self-pitying essay by a Canadian broadcaster, Jian Ghomeshi, who lost his job after more than twenty women accused him of slapping, punching, biting and choking them. The 'justification' for publishing the piece was that Ghomeshi had been cleared, in March 2016, of assaults on three women, while a further charge was dropped after he agreed to apologise to a former colleague. With so many allegations outstanding, the decision to publish was unwise to say the least, creating a furore in which the editor of the *NYRB* resigned. But the striking thing about the row was the number of well-known people who rushed to the editor's defence, some of them claiming that the #MeToo movement had gone too far. The backlash was predictable, given the number of famous men who found themselves fielding accusations of sexual harassment, sexual assault and rape, but the chief complaint – that so few allegations had been tested in court – was disingenuous in the extreme. The comedian Bill Cosby, who was one of the first men to go to prison as the movement got off the ground, was convicted on charges of drugging and sexual assault that were first reported to the police *thirteen years earlier*. A culture of impunity exists in the US and elsewhere, leaving women in little doubt that even allegations of serious male violence are unlikely to be believed.

In the UK, in the rare event of a sexual assault case going to court, prosecutors are up against two of the most common myths about rape, which are that woman can't be trusted to tell the truth and that men need to be protected from dishonest and vindictive accusers. The reality is that false accusations are rare: in a fourteen-month period analysed by the Crown Prosecution Service (CPS) in 2012, there were only thirty-five prosecutions for false allegations, compared with 5,651 prosecutions for rape.[194] Rape is very often a serial crime but the vast majority of rapists are never even prosecuted, let alone convicted. John Worboys, the black-cab rapist, is believed to have targeted more than a hundred women in London before he was finally convicted in 2009 for attacks on twelve women, and even then two of his victims had to go to court in 2018 to prevent his early release.

In 2017, the year when a record number of rape convictions were recorded in England and Wales, the grand total was still only 2,991.[195] To put that figure in perspective, the number of rapes recorded by the police *in London alone* in the same year was 7,095, and most experts think that represents only a fraction of the total.[196] The belief that women lie about rape was embedded in draconian new rules on disclosure of evidence which came into effect at the end of 2017, requiring complainants to provide access to the entire contents of their mobile phones, home and work computers, medical records and school and college records. The impact of this degree of intrusion, which may well breach a woman's right to private life under the European Convention on Human Rights, was immediately evident in crime statistics, which showed a 9.1 per cent fall in rape cases referred to the CPS and a 23.1 per cent drop in the number of cases that led to charges.[197] In a world where the true extent of male violence was recognised, such treatment of women and girls who have suffered brutal assaults would be a scandal – but we don't live in that world.

Domestic abuse is more common than rape but it remains vastly under-reported, as I showed in chapter two. Recent innovations in police procedure, such as recording call-outs to domestic incidents on body-worn cameras, have yet to improve the conviction rate; in 2017, domestic violence convictions in England and Wales actually *fell* from just over 87,000 to 84,565.[198] In Sweden, which is so often a pioneer in such matters, the criminal justice system long ago recognised that domestic abuse involves an accumulation of acts – not a single assault – which taken together amount to an offence of violating a woman's integrity. This is a significant development not just because it increases the odds of getting convictions, but because it undermines the myth of the gentle man who uncharacteristically lashes out.

Sadly, the UK lags far behind Sweden and British victims are rendered invisible along with the crime, forcing thousands of women to sleep on friends' sofas, risk homelessness or remain in violent relationships because the state doesn't provide enough refuge places. Politicians have a great deal to answer for on this score – not least Theresa May, whose frequently stated commitment to tackle the scourge of domestic violence, first as Home Secretary and then as Prime Minister, was accompanied by savage cuts to both police numbers and the funding of local authorities which are the principal source of grants for women's refuges. Many of the services provided to victims, such as specialist forms of counselling for women who have suffered extreme domestic abuse, are non-statutory – councils aren't legally obliged to offer them – and have been among the first to go when budgets are cut. These decisions may seem like one-offs but their effects are far-reaching, both for the well-being of victims who don't get the support they need and because they contribute to the *continuing invisibility* of violence against women. One of the consequences is that even manifestly violent men often don't end up with convictions, making them appear a great deal more harmless than they really are – and a small but significant proportion of those men will go on to commit terrorist attacks.

The hidden cost of male violence

One of the most damaging effects of normalising male violence is that we don't recognise it when it is staring us in the face. Terrorism is currently the most spectacular form of violence afflicting Western democracies, yet more often than not it is discussed as though it doesn't even belong in the category of male violence. For all sorts of reasons, people prefer to think that terrorism is solely about ideology, whether it's inspired by an extreme version of religion or the politics of the far right. It has become conventional among sections of the left to blame the terrorist attacks of the last decade on the invasion of Iraq, as though no further explanation for such extreme acts of male violence is needed; the hard right, meanwhile, has utilised terrorism to create fear and suspicion of Muslims, refugees and people from the BAME community generally.

These ideas have become entrenched, so much so that the proposition that terrorism has roots in the family and misogyny is likely to prompt angry denials, not least among men on the hard left ('brocialists') who pay lip service to feminism. Even some usually reasonable commentators see it as playing down the influence of Salafist forms of Islam, as though even to suggest that terrorism has deeper roots is letting the resurgence of fundamentalist forms of religion off the hook. Then there are those people who believe in 'noble cause' terrorism and argue that, while the methods of terrorists are reprehensible, they've been driven to it by colonialism, injustice and Western foreign policy. Both groups are unduly influenced by what terrorists say about themselves, even when it's a confused mess of propaganda, self-justification and self-aggrandisement. This book is full of examples of disturbed, angry men who had no insight into the causes of their rage – and might not have acted upon it if they had been remotely self-critical or introspective.

Obviously ideology plays a part in recruiting terrorists, but the question that doesn't get asked often enough is *why* some men are so susceptible to inflammatory rhetoric and sadistic videos. In the 1930s, hundreds of idealistic young men and women from the UK went to Spain to fight for the republican government, which was trying to survive a coup d'état staged by a fascist general, Francisco Franco. Similarly, a number of British volunteers, including former soldiers, have gone to Syria to fight with the Free Syrian Army or Kurdish forces opposing the Assad dictatorship. Like their predecessors, they went primarily for political or humanitarian reasons and they are, for the most part, a world apart from the violent young men who joined the al-Nusra Front or ISIS. The sheer number of sadists who became jihadists before the collapse of ISIS, gloating in videos as they stood next to mangled corpses or held up severed human heads, confirms how successfully modern terrorist organisations have targeted young men who *like* the idea of rape, torture and murder. As this book has shown, a substantial number of European recruits to ISIS were petty crooks with little interest in religion or politics until they encountered the incendiary propaganda of a terrorist group, and discovered they now had a 'reason' for the violence (often gang-related) that was already part of their lives.

It's clear that many people recoil from the idea that a proportion of men are drawn to violence, that some individuals gravitate towards extremist organisations precisely because they offer the opportunity to avenge past slights and exercise power over total strangers by hurting and killing them. It's a more controversial proposition than it should be, given that the history of earlier generations of terrorists supports it. During the 'Troubles' in Northern Ireland, members of paramilitary organisations on both sides became notorious for carrying out 'punishment beatings', a euphemism for vicious attacks, often on members of their own communities, which peaked at 326 in 1996 – almost one a day. Victims were savagely beaten, shot in the knees – hence the term 'kneecapping' – or had their limbs crushed with concrete blocks. The number of attacks fell over the next couple of years but began to rise again at the beginning of 1999, a few months after the signing of the Good Friday agreement which had led to hopes of an end to violence in Northern Ireland. Drawing attention to the increase, an article in the *Economist* suggested that the reason was nothing to do with ideology: 'The current increase in punishment attacks is probably related to the absence of other outlets for the "men of violence". None of the paramilitary groups has disbanded. "Punishments" are *the work of idle hands*.' [My italics][199]

Members of Black September, the Palestinian terrorist group responsible for the abduction of eleven Israeli athletes at the Munich Olympics in 1972, beat, shot and tortured their captives in the Olympic village before killing the surviving hostages during a botched escape attempt; it emerged in 2015 that one of the athletes, a weightlifter called Yossef Romano, was castrated either immediately before or just after his murder.[200]

Sabri Khalil al-Banna, better known by his nom de guerre Abu Nidal and probably the most feared Palestinian terrorist in the second half of the twentieth century, was a sadist and misogynist who was as notorious for torturing and killing members of his own organisation as he was for attacking Israeli targets. In the late 1980s, he is said to have ordered the murders of hundreds of members of the Abu Nidal Organisation, including

300 who were blindfolded, machine-gunned and pushed into trenches on a single night in south Lebanon. His biographer, Patrick Seale, traced Abu Nidal's 'bitter and vengeful' personality back to the humiliations he experienced during his childhood in Jaffa, in what was then Palestine. His elderly father, Khalil al-Banna, already had eleven children by his first wife when he became infatuated with his sixteen-year-old maid and married her. It doesn't sound as though the girl had much choice in the matter and the rest of the family were furious, as Seale explained:

> From the beginning, Sabri's position in the household was uncomfortable. He was scorned by his older half-brothers and -sisters. Worse still, when his father died in 1945, his mother was eventually turned out of the house and so he lost her too. Aged eight, Sabri remained in the parental home, but there was no one to care for him, and such neglect meant that he received virtually no education.[201]

The 'manifestos' and 'martyrdom videos' left behind by a new generation of terrorists *and* mass murderers tell us about their fantasies, their grievances and their hunger for fame (the latter being a common motivation for both groups) but not much else. Most commentators don't take the rambling diatribes of Elliot Rodger or Seung-Hui Cho at face value, but a terrorist has only to shout '*Allahu Akbar*' to close down any sensible discussion of what motivated him. By definition, terrorists are not thoughtful individuals with a critical interest in their unconscious thought processes, and the reluctance of the media to look beyond what appears on the surface is troubling.

The most egregious recent example is the Manchester Arena bombing which, while carried out by an Islamist, deliberately targeted teenage and younger girls. Nazir Afzal, then chief executive of the Association of Police and Crime Commissioners, wanted to put out a statement the following day, identifying it as a misogynistic attack, but he couldn't get the agreement of his board. I was invited to talk about the bombing on *Woman's Hour*, later in the same week, because the producers were puzzled by a widespread failure to connect it to ISIS's well-known record of extreme misogyny.

More than a year later, at the Labour Party conference in 2018, one of Jeremy Corbyn's closest aides, Andrew Murray, linked the attack to 'foreign policy', claiming, 'it has contributed to the environment in which these sort of atrocities continue to take place'.[202] Murray, who is a former chair of the Stop the War Coalition, did not explain why the British government's decision to take military action against Ramadan Abedi's arch enemy, Colonel Gaddafi, had motivated his son to blow the limbs off young girls in the city that had given his family refuge. There is a set of assumptions here that Afzal, who now advises the Welsh government on reducing violence against women, has observed with frustration. 'They would rather believe it was driven by politics than what it was really driven by,' he told me when we discussed the Manchester Arena bombing. He has sometimes felt like a lone voice, insisting on the relationship between terrorism, domestic violence and misogyny – and that the failure to recognise it is hampering counterterrorism efforts.

In December 2017, as David Anderson QC published his interim report into three of that year's successful terrorist attacks, the scale of the threat to the UK was spelled out for the first time by MI5. The figures were alarming, revealing that counterterrorism police and the security service had thwarted no fewer than twenty-two terrorist attacks in the previous four years. There were 'well over' 500 counterterrorism investigations under way, involving more than 3,000 SOIs (the 'subjects of interest' we met in earlier chapters of this book). In addition, there was 'a growing pool' of more than 20,000 individuals who had previously been the subject of terrorism investigations but were no longer considered an active threat. According to MI5: 'These investigations cover the full range of terrorist activity, from attack planning to activity that supports or facilitates terrorism – but a significant proportion involve potential attack planning threats. The tempo is more intense than ever.'[203]

It isn't difficult to imagine the huge demand in terms of the resources – case officers, communications experts and role players – needed to monitor 3,000 suspects who might be planning an imminent atrocity. There is also the difficulty, highlighted in some of the attacks described earlier in this book, of deciding when a 'closed' SOI such as Salman Abedi or Khalid Masood should become part of an active investigation again. In the introduction, I cited analysis from the Anderson report suggesting that a little under two-fifths of individuals convicted of terrorist offences in the UK were previously known to the police. Yet *most* of the terrorists, mass murderers and suspects I've written about in this book – Darren Osborne, Khalid Masood, Salman Abedi, Mohamed Lahouaiej-Bouhlel, Stephen Paddock, Seung-Hui Cho, Rachid Redouane, Jarrod Ramos, Kevin Neal, Ahmad Khan Rahimi, Robert Dear Jnr, Man Haron Monis, Devin Kelley, Tamerlan Tsarnaev, Omar Mateen, Nikolas Cruz and Driss Oukabir – had a record of abusing women. Just as striking, as I pointed out in chapter seven, is how few of these reports of domestic violence, stalking and even rape resulted in criminal convictions, let alone prison sentences. It's hard to know whether police and prosecutors truly understand the risks they're taking when they decide not to prosecute cases of domestic and sexual violence, leaving men free to attack other women – and, crucially, allowing them to maintain an unblemished record.

The proposition that the seriousness of male violence is consistently underestimated is borne out by the treatment of men like Theodore Johnson, the British serial killer I mentioned in chapter two, who got off with two manslaughter convictions involving domestic partners and was released to murder a third. In a climate where the outcome of going to the police is so uncertain, many women feel they have little choice but to take alternative measures, such as enlisting the help of friends and relatives, to get themselves out of a dangerous situation. In previous chapters, I described how Khalid Masood's first wife moved hundreds of miles to escape his violence while Rachid Redouane's wife left him, taking their baby daughter, and Omar Mateen's first wife was rescued by her parents.

What this means needs to be spelled out: time and time again, women are having to come up with *private* solutions to matters that should be dealt with by the criminal justice system. As Nazir Afzal has pointed out, the female relatives of extremists are often their first victims, to which I would add that domestic violence is a useful apprenticeship for men who are planning to crush passers-by under the wheels of an SUV or stab strangers with kitchen knives; men who have become desensitised to violence in the home are very dangerous, especially when they further dull their reactions by using steroids, as did both the Westminster Bridge and London Bridge attackers.

'Twenty-five thousand are at risk,' says Afzal, rounding up the number of individuals on the radar of police and the security services, 'and you can't monitor twenty-five thousand. But you shouldn't have to. You already know which ones to target by flagging up violence against women as a high-risk factor.' He is right: a history of abusing wives, girlfriends and other female relatives should send up a red flag when a man is being investigated for showing an interest in ISIS propaganda or far-right organisations. But that depends, to a large degree, on the authorities knowing about that history – and *that* depends on police reports and convictions.

Tackling violence against women – and terrorism

When I first began thinking and writing about this subject, a senior police officer said something very striking: 'Every day, my officers go into homes where a three-year-old boy has seen his mother being beaten up, and I know that we will probably be involved with that boy in ten or fifteen years' time.' The impact of ACEs is being recognised much more widely in the criminal justice system; to take just one example, the Ayrshire division of Police Scotland announced in 2018 that it was going to adopt a 'trauma-informed' approach to policing, citing research that suggested violent crime could be cut by half by tackling ACEs. The NHS argues that violence is a public-health issue, suggesting that it is as contagious as some diseases, and advocates programmes that support troubled families, encourage children's ability to form healthy relation-ships and work with teenagers who are at risk as victims and perpetrators.[204] The current Mayor of London, Sadiq Khan, set up a Violence Reduction Unit in 2018 which will focus on early interventions involving schools, healthcare professionals, local councils and the police – but that only applies to London. National government policy, by contrast, is neither moral nor effective, letting down victims and incurring huge costs further down the line when children who have grown up in abusive households get into trouble with the police as young adults.

Perpetrator programmes, designed to get violent men to change their behaviour, are not widely available and they're also controversial; women know that their abusers are manipulative, more than willing to sound contrite if it means getting access to children and the family home. Very often, perpetrator programmes compete for funds with organisations that support victims of domestic abuse, which desperately need money to provide safe accommodation and independent domestic-violence advisers (IDVAs).

Any serious attempt to reduce currently unacceptable levels of domestic violence would start with the following:

— Challenge the hugely damaging myth that women exaggerate and lie about the abuse they're suffering.
— Recognise domestic violence as a hidden epidemic, affecting every section of society, and a significant barrier to equality.
— Persuade more men to speak out against domestic abuse, challenging toxic notions of masculinity that link being a man with violence.
— Promote understanding of the link between domestic abuse and other forms of male violence, up to and including terrorism.
— Improve training for police officers and prosecutors to make sure that more cases of domestic abuse *and* rape result in convictions – and appropriate sentences.

— Provide better support for victims through the court process, including training and paying for more IDVAs, to reduce the currently high attrition rate.

— Create a compulsory register for individuals convicted of domestic violence, on the model of the sex offenders register. Improve the working of Clare's Law to make it easier for a woman to find out if a new partner is on it.

— Consult BAME women's organisations about how best to help women from ethnic minorities who may be isolated, unable to speak English and under family pressure not to report abuse – or signs of radicalisation.

— Make greater use of existing legislation such as domestic violence protection orders (DVPOs), which allow police and magistrates to remove perpetrators from the home for up to twenty-eight days, and change the law so that breaching a DVPO is a criminal offence.

— Bring the number of refuge spaces in line with demand, ensuring that women and children aren't trapped in violent homes or at risk of becoming homeless.

— Treat child witnesses as *victims* of domestic violence and ensure that they get support from specially trained social workers.

— Persuade schools to sign up to schemes where children feel safe to talk to teachers about what is happening at home, encouraging disclosure of abuse.

Intervening in families on this scale would be expensive and, in some quarters, controversial. But the costs of *not* dealing with domestic abuse have to be measured in terms of broken families, damaged women and children, prison sentences – and occasional acts of horrific public violence.

Terrorism is not inevitable: there are periods when it subsides until a new cause or organisation comes up with a fresh set of reasons to encourage the murder of complete strangers. Ideology plays a part but at a late stage in the process when it exploits angry men, encouraging them to deflect their low self-esteem and suicidal impulses on to strangers. Any vulnerable group can serve as scapegoats – women, Jews, Muslims, black people – but interventions need to start much earlier if we are to reduce the pool of recruits available to the next generation of terrorists.

The warning signs are there long before a man picks up a gun, hires a van or straps on a suicide vest, but they're to be found in the home – and too many of us are accustomed to looking the other way. If we want to stop mass murder in public places, we need to listen to the wives, girlfriends, mothers and sisters who have personal experience of dangerous, unstable men. Above all, we have to start believing women when they reveal the violence that is taking place every single day behind closed doors.

Acknowledgements

This was not an easy book to write, for obvious reasons, and I wouldn't have been able to finish it without the support and encouragement of a number of people. Claire Cohen, women's editor of the *Daily Telegraph*, commissioned a number of articles from me on the link between terrorism and domestic violence, and Anita Bennett urged me to expand my ideas into a book. I'm grateful to Jon Riley at riverrun for understanding why I wanted to write it, and to Rose Tomaszewska for her sympathetic and helpful editing suggestions.

For the last six years, I've worked closely with the VAWG team at the Mayor's Office for Policing and Crime at City Hall in London, especially Jain Lemom, and their research and experience have been invaluable in shaping my understanding of domestic violence. From the Metropolitan Police,

Commander Richard Smith and Deputy Commissioner Sir Craig Mackey helped further my knowledge of the impact of adverse childhood experiences on young offenders, offering some revealing insights into the formation of teenage gangs. Nazir Afzal's work on VAWG has long been an inspiration, and I was thrilled to meet and talk to him during the writing of the book. Mark Hosenball's knowledge of the UK security services and Islamist gangs was invaluable when I was researching the history of the London Boys.

Finally, I would like to thank friends who helped in different ways when the weight of the material was almost too much to bear: Maggie Huddleston, Laurel Playford, Anna Tymoshenko, Adnan Raunić, Dzenana Raunić and Alexander Seale. I am especially grateful to Rana Kabbani, who believed in this project more passionately than anybody.

Notes

Introduction

1   'Mass murderers have one thing in common – and it's not a "women's problem"', *Telegraph*, 20 July 2016
2   'The seeds of terrorism are often sown in the home – with domestic violence', *Guardian*, 10 July 2017

The Unassuageable Rage of the Kouachi Brothers

3   '"Charlie Hebdo": les femmes de la famille Kouachi témoignent', *Le Point*, 20 February 2015
4   'Recounting a Bustling Office at Charlie Hebdo, Then a "Vision of Horror"', *New York Times*, 8 January 2015
5   'Paris attacks: These troubled men who project their self-hatred onto others', *Independent on Sunday*, 11 January 2015
6   *Terror in France: The Rise of Jihad in the West*, Gilles Kepel with Antoine Jardin, Princeton University Press, 2017, p.xii

7   *Le Point*, op. cit., 20 February 2015

8   'L'enfance misérable des frères Kouachi', Reporterre website, 15 January 2015

9   Ibid.

10   *Jihad and Death: The Global Appeal of Islamic State*, Olivier Roy, translated by Cynthia Schoch, Hurst & Co., 2017, p.5

11   'From Amateur to Ruthless Jihadist in France', *New York Times*, 17 January 2015

Everything You Need to Know About Domestic Violence

12   'Domestic abuse in England and Wales: year ending March 2017', Office for National Statistics

13   Domestic violence information leaflet from Victim Support, January 2015

14   'Domestic abuse from a BME perspective', Bawso, 2010

15   ONS, op. cit.

16   'Homicide in England and Wales: year ending March 2017', ONS, 8 February 2018

17   'Domestic abuse in London 2015/16', Ashley Herron, Helena McKinnon and Michael Keenan, Mayor of London's Office for Policing and Crime, May 2016, p.19

18   Herron et al., op. cit., p.20

19   'Intimate personal violence and partner abuse', ONS, 11 February 2016

20   Ibid.

21   Herron et al., op. cit, p.20

22   '137 Shades of Terrorism: French Jihadists Before the Courts', Marc Hecker, Institut Français des Relations Internationales, 10 April 2018

23   'Intimate personal violence and partner abuse', ONS, 11 February 2016

24   See, for example, 'Inquiry into Trends and Issues in Domestic Violence in NSW', Jan Barham, 2011

25   'Repeat Domestic Abuser Criminal Career Analysis', Herron et al., op. cit, p.24

26   'Our Father Killed Our Mum and Sister – But My Brother's Strength Saved Me', Luke Hart, *Huffington Post*, 22 April 2017

27   *Islington Gazette*, 5 January 2018

28   Ibid., 14 March 2018

29   'Teenagers who plotted Columbine-style attack at Yorkshire school jailed', Sky News website, 20 July 2018

30   Figures from the domestic violence charity Refuge, at www. refuge.org.uk

31   The Children's Commissioner's 2018 Report into Childhood Vulnerability, 4 July 2018

32   'Behind Closed Doors: The Impact of Domestic Violence on Children', UNICEF 2006, p.4

33   'Trauma-informed care in response to adverse childhood experiences', *Nursing Times*, 8 June 2018

34   'A Crying Shame', Children's Commissioner for England, 17 October 2018

35   The Children's Commissioner's 2018 Report into Childhood Vulnerability, op. cit.

36   'Children in Danger: Act to End Violence Against Children', UNICEF UK, 2014

37   'Heightened neural reactivity to threat in child victims of family violence', Eamon McCrory, Stéphane De Brito, Catherine Sebastian, Andrea Mechelli, Geoffrey Bird, Phillip Kelly, Essi Viding, in *Current Biology*, Vol. 21, Issue 23, 6 December 2011

How Abusers Become Terrorists

38 '"He was going to kill me": Minister's bodyguard tells of moment he shot Westminster attacker Khalid Masood dead', *Independent*, 10 October 2018

39 'Westminster attacker had record of increasingly violent attacks', *Guardian*, 15 May 2017

40 'Attacks in London and Manchester, March–June 2017: independent assessment of MI5 and police internal reviews', David Anderson QC, December 2017

41 'Ex-wife of London terror attacker "abused and controlled by psychopath who she finally fled from"', *Mirror*, 24 March 2017

42 'Khalid Masood criticises wife for not saying "there's any good in ISIS" in audio', Sky News website, 21 September 2018

43 'Westminster attacker told mother: "They'll say I'm a terrorist, I'm not"', *Guardian*, 19 December 2018

44 'Judge who jailed Finsbury Park terror attacker for life: "We must respond to evil with good"', *Independent*, 2 February 2018

45 '"Finsbury Park mosque attacker Darren Osborne told pub-goers he would kill all Muslims", court hears', *Evening Standard*, 23 January 2018

46 'I know Mums defend their kids but I won't', *Sun*, 20 June 2017

47 'Judge who jailed Finsbury Park terror attacker for life: "We must respond to evil with good"', op. cit.

48 'The chilling warning about Finsbury Park terrorist from Swindon Crown Court – 11 years ago', *East London & West Essex Guardian*, 2 February 2018

49 'Who is Darren Osborne? Everything we know about the Finsbury Park mosque suspect', *Daily Telegraph*, 21 June 2017

50 'Ex-wife Says Orlando Shooter Might Have Been Hiding Homosexuality From His Family', *Time* magazine, 15 June 2016

51 'Orlando Gunman's Wife Breaks Silence: "I Was Unaware"', *New York Times*, 1 November 2016

52 'Attacks in London and Manchester, March–June 2017: independent assessment of MI5 and police internal reviews', David Anderson QC, December 2017

53 'Wife's marriage hell to London Bridge terrorist – maniac beat her up, locked her in if she drank and demanded she wore a hijab', *Mirror*, 6 June 2017

54 'Married to a jihadi', *Sun*, 6 June 2017

55 London terrorist Rachid Redouane's ex has 'shed many tears', Sky News, 7 June 2017

56 'Jo Cox murder: Judge's sentencing remarks to Thomas Mair', BBC News website, 23 November 2016

57 'Thomas Mair: The far-right extremist who murdered MP Jo Cox', *Independent*, 23 November 2016

58 'The lasting mystery of the Tsarnaev brothers', CNN, 18 May 2015

59 'Former girlfriend of Boston bomber reveals he slapped her and beat her head against a car for wearing shorts', *Daily Mail*, 9 May 2013

60 Tsarnaev's connections: Who's who, CNN, 4 March 2015

61 Inquest into the deaths arising from the Lindt Café siege, findings and recommendations, State Coroner of New South Wales, May 2017, pp. 140-142

62 Ibid., p.129

63 Ibid., p.13

64 Ibid., p.61

65 Ibid., p.65

66   'The many faces of Lindt siege gunman Monis, Four Corners', ABC News, 22 May 2017

67   Inquest into the deaths arising from the Lindt Café siege, op. cit., p11

68   'Amirah Droudis jailed for stabbing murder of Lindt gunman Man Monis' ex-wife', *Sydney Morning Herald*, 1 February 2017

69   'Barcelona terrorist jailed for attacking girlfriend', thinkSPAIN website, 29 March 2018

70   'Nice attacker grew beard in week before truck attack – prosecutor', *Guardian*, 18 July 2016

From Children to Perpetrators

71   'Attacks in London and Manchester, March–June 2017: independent assessment of MI5 and police internal reviews', op. cit., p.16

72   Jihadist with links to Manchester bomber is guilty of fighting for Isis, *Guardian*, 7 December 2017

73   Ibid.

74   'The 2017 Attacks: What needs to change?' Intelligence and Security Committee report, 22 November 2018, p.33

75   Ibid., p.113

76   Ibid., p.92

77   'Navy rescued Manchester bomber Salman Abedi from wartorn Libya three years before deadly terror attack', *Telegraph*, 31 July 2018

78   'Manchester Arena bomber Salman Abedi 'went to college in Islamic dress and argued with any woman in authority', *Mirror*, 27 May 2017

79   'How Manchester bomber Salman Abedi was radicalised by his links to Libya', *Observer*, 28 May 2017

80   Intelligence and Security Committee report, op. cit., p.94

81   *Mirror*, op. cit., 27 May 2017

82   'Revealed: How the Manchester bomber was a dope-smoking and vodka-drinking party boy nicknamed Dumbo who said he had anger issues', *Daily Mail*, 25 May 2017

83   'Attacks in London and Manchester, March–June 2017: independent assessment of MI5 and police internal reviews', op. cit., p.27

84   'Italian officials alerted UK about Youssef Zaghba, says prosecutor', *Guardian*, 7 June 2017

85   Intelligence and Security Committee report, op. cit., p.78

86   'London Bridge terrorist's sister says they fell out over her wearing miniskirts as she says she won't go to the killer's funeral and wishes she could "beat him to a pulp"', *Daily Mail*, 20 June 2017

87   Ibid.

88   '"I'm just a sociopath," Dylann Roof declared after deadly church shooting rampage, court records say', *Washington Post*, 17 May 2017

89   'Dylann Roof: Experts believe Charleston shooting suspect was author of racist manifesto and "self-radicalised" online', *Independent*, 29 June 2015

90   'Charleston Shooting Suspect Was Drawn Into "Internet Evil", Relatives Say', *Time* magazine, 21 June 2015

91   'Mother and daughters guilty of plotting terrorist attacks', Metropolitan Police website, News, 4 June 2018

92   'All-female terror cell members jailed for knife attack plot', Sky News website, 15 June 2018

93   'The radicalisation of Safaa Boular: A teenager's journey to terror', BBC News website, 4 June 2018

94   Ibid.

95   'Teenager, Safaa Boular, found guilty of first all-female UK terror plot', Sky News website, 5 June 2018

96 'Members of all-female terror cell jailed over London knife plot', *Guardian*, 15 June 2018

97 'British ISIS fighter who was plotting a massacre on home soil is killed by a US drone in a secret UK-led mission in Syria', *Daily Mail*, 16 February 2018

98 BBC News website, op. cit., 4 June 2018

99 'Syed Farook and Tashfeen Malik: What we know about the San Bernardino shooters', *Telegraph*, 5 December 2015

100 'San Bernardino Shooter's Father Had History of Domestic Violence, Alcoholism', The Fix website, 4 December 2015

101 'Brighton fighter Amer Deghayes still alive and well in Syria', Brighton *Argus*, 24 September 2018

102 Much of the information regarding the family comes from the serious case review by Edi Carmi and Anna Gianfrancesco, published by the Brighton & Hove Local Safeguarding Board on 27 July 2017

103 Ibid., p.12

104 Ibid., p.13

105 'From Brighton to the battlefield: how four young Britons were drawn to jihad', *Guardian*, 31 March 2016

106 Safeguarding Board review, op. cit., p.13

107 Ibid., p.13

108 Ibid., p.28

109 Ibid., pp.61–2

110 Ibid., p.15

111 Ibid., pp.61–2

112 'Imam backs terror attack against Blair', *Sunday Times*, 18 June 2006

113 Safeguarding Board review, op. cit., p.50

114 Ibid., p.51

115 Brighton *Argus*, op. cit., 24 September 2018

The World's Biggest Gang

116 'The mental health needs of gang-affiliated young people', Public Health England, 27 January 2015, p.7

117 'Gangs: Don't you know it's different for girls', Nicola Weller, published in Respect newsletter, January 2010

118 Ibid., p.8

119 'Criminal Pasts, Terrorist Futures: European Jihadists and the New Crime–Terror Nexus', Rajan Basra, Peter Neumann and Claudia Brunner, ICSR, 2016, p.7

120 'Leaked Isis documents reveal recruits have poor grasp of Islamic faith', Independent, 16 August 2016

121 'Germany searches for IS member behind Anis Amri's Berlin truck attack', Deutsche Welle website, 5 July 2018

122 'Woolwich killing: what made two gang members turn to jihad?' Observer, 26 May 2013

123 'A Brussels Mentor Who Taught "Gangster Islam" to the Young and Angry', New York Times, 11 April 2016

124 Ibid.

125 Basra et al., ICSR, op. cit., p.26

126 'Brussels jihadists: Belgian recruiter Zerkani given longer term', BBC News website, 14 April 2016

127 Basra et al., ICSR, op. cit., pp.26–7

128 'Fertile Ground for Militancy in Hometown of "Jihadi John"', New York Times, 28 February 2015

129 Case no: PTA/4/2011, High Court of Justice, Queen's Bench Division, 21 December 2011

130 'Mohammed Emwazi was pawn in Isis's stupid game, says victim's daughter', Guardian, 13 November 2015

131 'Who is Mohammed Emwazi? From shy, football-loving boy to Isis killer', Guardian, 13 November 2015

132 'Jihadi John "kidnapped two teenagers at gunpoint and dumped them beside M1 in their underwear in revenge for attacking his brother"', *Evening Standard*, 5 March 2015

133 US State Department Terrorist Designation of Alexanda Amon Kotey, Bureau of Counterterrorism and Countering Violent Extremism, 10 January 2017

134 'Mother who tried to send cash in friend's knickers to jihadist husband in Syria is jailed', *Daily Telegraph*, 13 November 2014

135 US State Department Terrorist Designation of El Shafee Elsheikh, Bureau of Counterterrorism and Countering Violent Extremism, 30 March 2017

136 The most detailed account of El Shafee Elsheikh's background is to be found in a Buzzfeed News investigation by Jane Bradley: 'My Son The ISIS Executioner', 23 May 2016

Misogyny Inc.

137 'Whose fault is the jihadist bride? Certainly not her astonishing dad', *Spectator*, 11 April 2015

138 'If teenage girls want to join Isis in the face of all its atrocities, then they should leave and never return', *Independent*, 23 February 2015

139 'The jihadist girls who went to Syria weren't just radicalised by Isis – they were groomed', *Independent*, 25 February 2015

140 'Women of the Islamic State: A manifesto on women by the Al-Khanssaa Brigade', translation and analysis by Charlie Winter, Quilliam Foundation, February 2015, p.18

141 Ibid., p.27

142 'German girl imprisoned for Isis role has fleeting family reunion', *Guardian*, 15 December 2017

143 ‘"Till Martyrdom Do Us Part": Gender and the ISIS Phenomenon', Erin Saltman and Melanie Smith, Institute for Strategic
Dialogue, 2015, p.4

144 'From Daesh to "Diaspora": Tracing the Women and Minors of
Islamic State', Joana Cook and Gina Vale, ICSR, 2018, p.3

145 *Two Sisters: Into the Syrian Jihad*, Åsne Seierstad, Virago, 2018,
p.345

146 'Isis Austrian poster girl Samra Kesinovic "used as sex slave"
before being murdered for trying to escape', *Independent*, 31
December 2015

147 'Isis bride Shamima Begum: "When I saw my first severed head
it didn't faze me at all" ', *The Times*, 13 February 2019.

148 Landmark Cases: 'Kunarac *et al.*: sexual enslavement and rape as
crimes against humanity', UN, International Residual Mechanism for Criminal Tribunals

149 'Conflict-Related sexual violence', Report of the Secretary General, UN Security Council, 23 March 2015, p.24

150 Ibid.

151 'Defected from ISIS or Simply Returned, and for How Long?
– Challenges for the West in Dealing with Returning Foreign
Fighters', Anne Speckhard, Ardian Shajkovci and Ahmet Yayla,
Homeland Security Affairs website, January 2018

152 'Rape and slavery was lure for UK Isis recruits with history of
sexual violence', *Observer*, 7 October 2017

153 'Mortality and kidnapping estimates for the Yazidi population in
the area of Mount Sinjar, Iraq, in August 2014: A retrospective
household survey', *PLOS Medicine*, 9 May 2017

154 'UN Commission of Inquiry on Syria: ISIS is committing
genocide against the Yazidis', UN Human Rights Office of the
High Commissioner, 16 June 2016

155 *The Girl Who Beat ISIS: My Story*, Farida Khalaf, with Andrea
Hoffmann, translated by Jamie Bulloch, Square Peg, 2016

156 Ibid., p.73

157 'Sharing His Sex Slave and Other Highlights From the Islamic State's Obituary for Jihadi John', *Foreign Policy* magazine, 18 January 2016

158 Excerpts published by the Middle East Media Research Institute, December 2014

159 'Wife of ISIS Figure Charged in American Woman Kayla Mueller's Death', ABC News website, 8 February 2016

160 'Nobel Peace Prize 2018 goes to Yazidi activist and Congolese gynaecologist', *Telegraph*, 5 October 2018

Angry White Men

161 'When Men Murder Women: An Analysis of 2015 Homicide Data', Violence Policy Center, September 2017, p.5

162 'American Roulette: Murder–Suicide in the United States' (sixth edition), Marty Langley, Violence Policy Center, June 2018

163 'Guns and Violence Against Women: America's Uniquely Lethal Domestic Violence Problem', Everytown for Gun Safety, 2014

164 'Transcript: President Obama at Sandy Hook Prayer Vigil', NPR website, 16 December 2012

165 'FBI documents reveal Newtown shooter Adam Lanza's pedophilia interest', CNN website, 27 October 2017

166 'Newly released FBI documents reveal disturbing details about Sandy Hook shooter Adam Lanza, *USA Today*, 25 October 2017

167 'In 2012 Assault, Texas Gunman Broke Skull of Infant Stepson', *New York Times*, 6 November 2017

168 'Gunman in Northern California rampage was not supposed to have guns', CNN website, 16 November 2017

169 'California shooting gunman was "paranoid", DA says', CNN, 16 November 2017

170 'Killer's manifesto: "You forced me into a corner"', CNN website, 18 April 2007

171 'What the Planned Parenthood Shooter Wanted', *Atlantic*, 12 April 2016

172 'Accused Planned Parenthood Shooter: "I'm A Warrior For The Babies"', NPR website, 9 December 2015

173 'For Robert Dear, Religion and Rage Before Planned Parenthood Attack', *New York Times*, 1 December 2015

174 'Colorado Springs shooter Robert L. Dear was an accused Peeping Tom once arrested for animal cruelty', *Daily Caller*, 28 November 2015

175 *New York Times*, op. cit., 1 December 2015

176 'My Twisted World: The Story of Elliot Rodger', Elliot Rodger, p.101

177 Ibid., p.121

178 'When a Mass Murderer Has a Cult Following', *The Cut* magazine, 27 April 2018

179 'Elliot Rodger: How misogynist killer became "incel hero"', BBC News website, 26 April 2018

180 'Santa Fe school shooting suspect "spared victims to tell his story"', BBC, 20 May 2018

181 'Texas school shooting victim's mother says daughter rejected suspect's advances', CBS News website / Associated Press, 20 May 2018

182 'Las Vegas gunman Stephen Paddock paid off all his debts before shooting 58 people dead, new report reveals', *Newsweek*, 19 January 2018

183 'Vegas gunman liked "violent" rape fantasies, prostitute says', *New York Post*, 8 October 2017

184 '"He sent her away so she didn't interfere with what he was planning": Sisters of Las Vegas gunman's girlfriend break silence

saying "only she can put the puzzle together" over possible motive for the tragic massacre', *Daily Mail*, 4 October 2017

185 'Killer's boast to hooker: Hooker reveals how Las Vegas gunman Stephen Paddock acted out violent rape fantasies and bragged: "I was born bad"', *Sun on Sunday*, 8 October 2017

186 'A psychological evaluation of the Las Vegas gunman's criminal father could offer clues about the shooter's psyche', Business Insider website, 13 October 2017

187 'Las Vegas shooter's father was on FBI's Most Wanted list and called "psychopathic"', Miami Herald, 2 October 2017

188 '"Most dangerous person I've ever dealt with": Lawyer feared newspaper murder suspect, USA Today, 30 June 2018

189 'Florida school shooting suspect hid among students after massacre', CBS News website, 15 February 2018

190 'School shooter showed violence and mental instability at home, police reports reveal', CNN, 17 February 2018

191 'Social media paints picture of racist "professional school shooter"', CNN, 15 February 2018

Terrorism Begins at Home

192 'A proposed Ohio law would redefine a person to include "unborn humans" and could treat abortion like murder', CNN website, 21 November 2018

193 'The Cruelty is the Point', *Atlantic*, 3 October 2018

194 'Rape and Sexual Offences', Chapter 21: Societal Myths, Myth 7, CPS website

195 'CPS report shows more offenders are being successfully prosecuted for sexual crimes than ever before', CPS News Centre website, 10 October 2017

196 Violence Against Women and Girls dashboard, Mayor of Lon-

don's Office for Policing and Crime, rolling year to September 2017

197 'Annual Violence against Women and Girls report published', CPS News Centre website, 26 September 2018

198 Ibid.

199 'The beating goes on', *Economist*, 28 January 1999

200 'Long-Hidden Details Reveal Cruelty of 1972 Munich Attackers', *New York Times*, 1 December 2015

201 *Abu Nidal, A Gun for Hire: the Secret Life of the World's Most Notorious Arab Terrorist*, Patrick Seale, Random House, 1992, p.58

202 'Corbyn aide Andrew Murray's Manchester Arena bomb speech condemned', *Times*, 25 September 2018

203 'Publication of David Anderson QC's report on the terrorist attacks of March–June 2017', News and Speeches, MI5 website, 5 December 2017

204 'Protecting People, Promoting Health: A public health approach to violence prevention for England', Mark Bellis, Karen Hughes, Clare Perkins and Andrew Bennett, North West Public Health Observatory at the Centre for Public Health, Liverpool John Moores University, NHS / Department of Health, October 2012

Index